THE CATHEDRAL
OF REIMS ૭

IMPRIMATUR

    EDM. CAN. SURMONT,

               Vic. Gen.

NIHIL OBSTAT

    FR. INNOCENTIUS APAP., O.P.

             Censor Deputatus.

      Westmonasterii, die 23 Decembris, 1919.

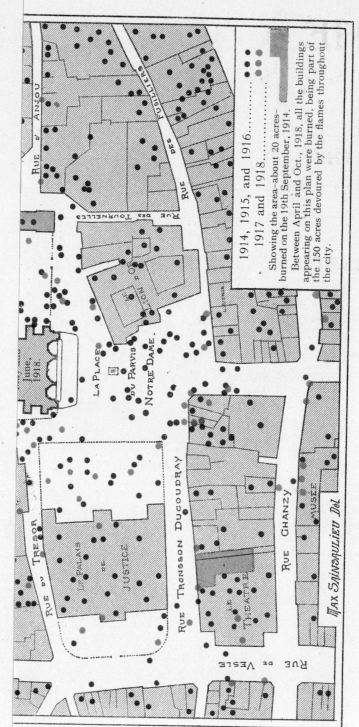

1914, 1915, and 1916............. ● ● ●
1917 and 1918............. ● ● ●

Showing the area—about 20 acres—
burned on the 19th September, 1914.
Between April and Oct., 1918, all the buildings
appearing on this plan were burned, being part of
the 150 acres devoured by the flames throughout
the city.

RUE D' ANJOU

RUE DES FUSILLIERS

RUE DES TOURNELLES

June, 1918

LA PLACE
DU PARVIS
NOTRE DAME.

RUE DU TRESOR

RUE TRONSSON DUCOUDRAY

LE PALAIS DE JUSTICE

LE THEATRE

RUE CHANZY

MUSEE

RUE DE VESLE

MAX SAINSAULIEU Del.

THE CATHEDRAL OF REIMS

THE STORY OF A GERMAN CRIME

BY

THE RIGHT REVEREND

MONSEIGNEUR MAURICE LANDRIEUX

BISHOP OF DIJON

AND ARCHPRIEST OF REIMS CATHEDRAL 1912-1916

TRANSLATED BY

ERNEST E. WILLIAMS

BARRISTER-AT-LAW

Quod scimus loquimur,
Quod vidimus testamur.

Crowned by the French Academy

LONDON:

KEGAN PAUL, TRENCH, TRUBNER & CO., LTD.

NEW YORK: E. P. DUTTON & CO.

1920

CONTENTS

LIST OF ILLUSTRATIONS

vi

List of Illustrations

THE CATHEDRAL OF REIMS

FOR half a century Germany has been dominated by two forms of pride—military ambition and intellectual pedantry, the one engendering the other. She carried self-esteem and self-admiration to such a pitch that she believed herself, and told herself, that she was a nation without peer, a people-type marked out to be the head of the human race. She made herself a soldier that she might realize her dream, militarism being thus the servant of German Thought. She was to become " Greatest Germany," to extend ever farther afield, to mount ever higher, by force of arms and the spread of her culture : *Deutschland über alles*, Germany before all and above all, was to dominate everywhere, and to rule the world.

She had brought into being a formidable engine of war. She produced the illusion, or the impression, of a certain scientific superiority, ponderous and massive, like her soldiers, and like them also in strength. She paraded this achievement with such an air of assurance, with such haughtiness, such an accent of superb arrogance, that she imposed her conviction upon others.

And these two boasts fall simultaneously, in the same catastrophe : the military boast has been shattered, though not ingloriously, in those combats of giants such as humanity

B

has never hitherto witnessed ; the intellectual boast has foundered miserably amid orgies of cruelty, of villainies, of stupid malevolence, which are only to be matched in the worst periods of history, and are on a par with the vilest excesses of barbarian hordes.

The enormous power of the German armies and their monstrous engines of war astounded the world ; but their crimes have sickened it ; so that it is hard to say which feeling is uppermost—surprise at the obstinate resistance of the Kaiser's soldiers, or indignation at the savage destruction they have wrought.

Their unjustified devastation of Malines and Louvain, of Ypres, of Arras, of Senlis and Soissons and the Somme will never be forgotten ; and never will they be pardoned for their bombardment and burning of Reims Cathedral.

That was " the German Crime," which stands out in relief from among their other crimes—not the worst perhaps : their crimes have been many and atrocious—but the most ignoble, because it was at once sacrilegious and stupid, and because it reveals, by its uselessness, the blackest depth of German misdoing. That the idea of it should have germinated in the mind of the responsible master, or been suggested to him ; that it should have been possible to formulate it in high places, and discuss it in war councils ; that it could travel through German brains to the unreasoning hands of Prussian gunners and the cannon's mouth, and its course not be stayed by indignant protest ; that it should have been realized in cold blood, methodically, persistently ; that it should not have afterwards revolted opinion on the other side of the Rhine ; that not one voice from the high places of Germanic scholarship should have

2

Pl. 1

Photo Poirier

THE SHELL OF THE 4TH SEPTEMBER, 1914, IN THE UPPER GALLERY OF THE
NORTH TRANSEPT (see p. 17; face p. 2)

Photo Thinot

THE SMILING ANGEL, THE LIP INJURED (see p. 15)

Pl. 2

THE CATHEDRAL DOMINATING THE CITY *(see p. 18; face p. 3)*

dared to cry out its reprobation, to save at least the honour of the few—all this is more than proof enough of the bankruptcy of this " culture," more than enough to put this people under the ban of civilization.

.   .   .   .

The burning of Reims Cathedral was not a mere incident of war ; it was an outstanding event which excited anger and indignation throughout the whole world ; it is well, then, to preserve its full history—to the shame of Germany, and for ourselves as an act of pious remembrance.

The hurried and badly documented accounts which appeared in the Press were necessarily incomplete, and they were often fanciful ; they did not agree ; they even contradicted one another. It is not enough, for the proper description of a scene of this kind (as some have attempted, with quite disconcerting light-heartedness) to collate, at a distance, various newspaper articles and scraps of information collected at haphazard in conversation ; nor even, during a rapid visit, to handle the calcinated stones, and glance at the injuries which the building has suffered : the cold lava which one picks up on the mountain side gives no idea of the volcano. One must have followed, minute by minute, as we have done, each phase of the drama ; have had the vision of it constantly before one's eyes, have lived on the spot through those sinister hours, in order to reconstruct the scene, and to relate it with the precision as well as with the feeling which it demands.

Now, on the 19th of September and the preceding days we, *curé* and *vicaires*—those at least who were not with the army—were alone, with the German wounded, in the

Cathedral. It is upon us then that is imposed the duty of reassembling and co-ordinating the documents,[1] as in a *procès-verbal*, in order to set forth the history of those tragic days, and to rectify many inexactitudes, and to put an end to many misunderstandings : *quod scimus loquimur ; quod vidimus testamur* (John iii. 11).

The prolongation of the war, the position of the city of Reims in the firing-line, which for four years kept the Cathedral under the fire of the German batteries, as well as the rigour of the military censorship, have retarded the publication of this book, the first chapters of which were written in January, 1915. It was, besides, indispensable to wait until the end, and to know in what condition the last bombardment would leave our Cathedral, in order to trace a complete picture of the catastrophe.

M. LANDRIEUX.

---

[1] A third at least of the photographs reproduced in this book have been taken by M. l'Abbé Thinot, *maître de chapelle* at Notre Dame. He had watched over the Cathedral, with passionate solicitude, until his departure for the Army in January, 1915.

He was exempt from service, but he refused to avail himself of the exemption. He asked repeatedly, and eventually obtained, the post of military chaplain to the 34th Division of the 17th Corps.

His ardent nature, his almost foolhardy courage, his apostolic zeal predestined him for this mission. He consecrated himself to it unreservedly ; for, from the first day, he had made the sacrifice of his life.

On the 16th of March he fell, in the first line, struck by a bullet in the head, meriting the citation which he received in the Army Order of the day :—

" Abbé Remy Thinot, Chaplain :

Having gone into the trenches at the moment of an attack to perform his ministerial functions, he was there mortally wounded whilst going to the succour of soldiers buried under the débris of a mine explosion, and while exhorting the men to do their duty."

Pl. 3

Photo J. Matot

JOAN OF ARC IN THE MIDST OF THE GERMANS *(see p. 21; face p. 4)*

Pl. 4

Photo J. Matot

THE GREAT NAVE EMPTY, WITH THE FIRST TRUSSES OF STRAW (*see p. 23*)

Photo J. Matot

THE CHAIRS IN THE SANCTUARY (*see p. 23; face p. 5*)

THIS book, compiled in the course of the events it portrays, is a book written in good faith. I have often had to introduce information gathered from day to day in the Press. I have taken this information for what it was worth, and I am ready to rectify it if more precise documents show it to be inexact in any particular.

M. L.

I

THE MISTAKE OF THE 4TH OF SEPTEMBER?

CHAPTER I

THE MISTAKE OF THE 4TH OF SEPTEMBER?

FROM the beginning of the war the Cathedral has been associated with that fine impulse of patriotism which uplifted the country and carried our regiments to the frontier.

Each morning, up to his departure for the Conclave on Thursday the 24th of August,[1] Cardinal Luçon said Mass there for the Army ; and at the end of the day the faithful resorted thither in crowds for the Stations of the Cross, with the feeling that there that intercession took on the character and the grandeur of a national act of prayer.

But it is our soldiers who gave to Notre-Dame its final joys. The parochial office being ended, in the evening, when the softened tints of twilight had died away in the magic colours of the windows, they grouped themselves in compact masses at the foot of the pulpit. A priest—often a soldier priest[2]—spoke to them, in heart-felt language, of the great truths of the Faith, of the France for which they were sacrificing everything, even their blood, of Heaven, the other Motherland, where the sacrifice receives

---

[1] His Eminence was only able to re-enter Reims on the 22nd of September, three days after the catastrophe.

[2] M. l'Abbé Thellier de Poncheville (of the 1st Section of Infirmiers) has published, under the title of *The Last Prayers in the Cathedral of Reims*, his burning and vibrating addresses at our military reunions. (Paris, Rioud.)

its recompense. They prayed, they sang a hymn, and received the Benediction of the Blessed Sacrament. Then, against a pillar, or even in the naves, confessors took up their stations, and penitents fell upon their knees ; and more than once could be seen the spectacle of a soldier absolving an officer, perchance his lieutenant or his captain.

These military *réunions* came brusquely to an end upon the approach of the Germans.

Driven back ever further to the south, those lamentable exoduses of distracted people, urged on by fear, which poured down towards Reims, marked for us the stages of the invasion ; after Namur, after Charleroi, there were Givet and the valley of the Meuse, then Charleville, and soon Rethel. It was necessary that the Army should retire, bend its line once more, in accordance with the exigencies of that slow-moving strategy, that laborious, carefully-reasoned-out retreat, which depressed us with its appearance of defeat, but which prepared the victory of the Marne.

On the morning of the 4th of September, the XIIth Saxon Corps was at the gates of Reims. The advance guard had presented itself at the Hôtel de Ville the previous evening, and had passed the night there.

The way was free, the forts had been evacuated ; resistance would have been inopportune at the least : Reims declared itself an open town.

It was the first Friday of the month. I had finished my sermon at the Cathedral in these words—and they had been considered severe :

" *God will save us. But to the extent that in the providential order success will return to us, to that extent we must expect to pay dearly for it. . . . When the cyclone shall have passed our poor France will find herself, not standing forth in pride and glory, but on her knees, in mourning, amid ruins !* "[1]

An hour later a strange detonation was heard ; then a second ; a third. It appeared strange, but at first no great heed was paid to it. All the population was out of doors. It was thought that the Germans were blowing up the bridges, or perhaps that they were celebrating with salvos of artillery the anniversary of the battle of Sedan, the 4th of September, 1870. But the whistling sounds and the booming in the air soon brought back men's minds to reality.

At the third explosion a splinter of shell fell at my feet. It was in the Place Belletour. I knew then what it meant.

Without any warning, without any one knowing why, a savage bombardment was being launched upon the city.

Hastily, along streets become suddenly deserted, and appearing panic-stricken—everywhere doors closed and shutters barred—I went to the Cathedral, to watch over the Blessed Sacrament. Ten times at least the sinister whistle passed over my head while I was on the way.

The Place du Parvis, when I arrived there, was obscured in a thick cloud of dust and smoke, through which it was scarcely possible to distinguish the outline of the Palais de Justice : bombs had already fallen there, two paces from the entrance ; others were exploding on the surrounding houses.

For a moment, I admit, I had the thought, though I

[1] *Quelques Prônes de Guerre*, p. 20.

did not give way to it, of going back ; but I rushed through ; and when under the porch of the Cathedral I noticed that already there was debris of stone which had fallen from the coping.

I thought I was alone. After making a tour round the church I went to the Chapel of the Blessed Sacrament. One of my *vicaires*, M. l'Abbé Andrieux, had preceded me. He had taken refuge with an employé of the church, M. Huilleret, and some others, in the clock staircase, near the small entrance.

Soon afterwards a man,[1] who had run from the Hôtel de Ville, arrived breathless, with a sheet which had been hurriedly nailed to the stick of a Turk's-head broom. He and the *vicaire* courageously mounted to the north tower, and that white flag was unfurled in the wind. " The cannonade raged," wrote M. Andrieux, some days later. " The condition of the Cathedral was ominous. The church was full of smoke. Dust rose to the roof in opaque masses. . . . Glass from the windows crashed down upon the floors of the lower nave. . . . We get into the staircase. We climb it breathlessly. Arrived at the foot of the towers, we are stopped by a closed door ; for we are without the key. We unite our efforts to lift the door off its hinges. We arrive at the top, and, with tense feelings, we flourish the white flag. . . .

" Up there the spectacle was unique. Jets of smoke and dust in the town marked the places which were hit. Two shells fell on the house of M. Ch. Clignet, in the Rue de Trésor. We saw flames burst forth from M. J. Matot's house, at the corner of the Rue de la Salle. A volume of

---

[1] M. Rouné, a member of the Sauveteurs.

Pl. 5

THE STRAW SPREAD OUT IN THE NAVES *(see p. 23; face p. 12)*

Pl. 6

Photo Thinot

AFTER THE FIRE.
THE RED CROSS FLAG IS STILL FLOATING ON THE NORTH TOWER (see p. 27; face p. 13)

smoke marked the beginning of a fire in a block of factories close to the Rue Houzeau-Muiron. . . .

" At length the hurricane of iron and fire ceased. A German aeroplane flew for an instant over our heads, then wheeled round, and regained with all speed the heights of Pargny."[1]

Meanwhile the Saxon officers, who had believed at first that this was a counter-offensive of our own, more astonished than anyone at seeing themselves bombarded by their own guns—it was necessary to take them splinters of their own shells in order to convince them—had hurriedly sent two of their number with one of the city employés[2] in a motor-car, in the direction of the firing, to report and obtain a cessation of the bombardment. They found the batteries at Mesneux, seven kilometres from Reims.

It was another army corps—a Prussian corps, which was ignorant of the arrival of the Saxons, and had ruined the city on account of a couple of envoys.

Having set out for Reims the previous evening, two officers of the Prussian Guard—personages of weight, " who are worth more," declared Von Bülow's envoy, " than yon hundred thousand swine of Reims "—Messrs. von Arnim and von Kummer, had not reappeared. It had been concluded that they were prisoners ; and, without troubling to obtain further information, the city was made to suffer the consequences.

The truth was that, having arrived too late, the envoys, after a stop at La Neuvillette, had continued their journey by Thil, Pouillon, Merfy, to Epernay, in order to reach

[1] *Courrier de la Champagne*, 8th September, 1914.

[2] M. Charlier, sub-librarian.

13

the French lines, and that they had never set foot at all in Reims.[1]

That day there were nearly two hundred victims, of whom sixty were killed, besides the ruin in all parts of the city.

It had cost us dear, this " mistake " of the Prussian Guard ! For they pretended that it had been a mistake. But why, then, one asked, had Colonel von Roeder, who was in command of the battery at Mesneux, spoken to M. Brulé, the Mayor, of " a bombardment for purposes of intimidation " ?[2]

But, mistake or not, the mischief was done, and the Cathedral had already been struck.

Having been rejoined, about half-past ten, by M. l'Abbé Thinot, we together made a rapid exploration, to count the wounds, and ascertain the damage.

In the church a thick mist, charged with dust, mounts to the roof. Broken glass, scattered over the pavement, crackles beneath our feet ; pieces of twisted lead lie on the ground, with bits of iron torn from the window frames ; for, on the side abutting on the Rue Robert de Coucy, the lower windows are in a pitiable condition ; three are gutted, and entire panels have fallen. The last window, near the staircase of the tower, the only one which still

[1] M. Léon de Tassigny, Mayor of La Neuvillette, to whom they had applied on the 2nd September, then offered, with M. Kiener, to go through the German lines in search of them, in order to save the city from threatened reprisals. The Duke of Mecklenburg accompanied them as far as Montmirail. They only returned to Reims on the 15th of October, after an Odyssey of seventy days, during which they had been twenty times at close quarters with death.

Messrs. von Arnim and von Kummer, who had never been able to establish properly the official character of their mission, had been stopped and kept at Orleans. They were given their liberty towards the middle of October.

[2] He also said he had fired only 60 rounds ; but in fact 182 shells fell on the town, of which 56 did not explode. (Cf. *Le Martyre de Reims*, p. 80.)

14

Pl. 7

Photo Thinot

THE WINDOW GUTTED BY A SHELL (ON THE RIGHT) THE *DÉBRIS* OF WHICH
KILLED THREE MEN, ON THE FRIDAY MORNING (*see p. 28; face p. 14*)

Pl. 8

Photo L. Dage

THE SCAFFOLDING ON FIRE (see *p.* 39; *face p.* 15)

retains a vestige of the ancient glass of the Thirteenth century, has been injured in this precious spot.

The large window by the pointed spandrel of the porch, above the lobby, has been cut on one side. The Great Rose is perforated in several places. Lower down, the old windows of the gallery, in the triforium, have been shaken ; that on the left is in pieces. The Small Rose (of the Eighteenth century) is riddled, especially in the upper part.

But our search reveals no traces of explosions within the church, as we had feared. We therefore continue our inspection outside.

The courtyard of the front is strewn with small debris of stones and sculptures. We pick up the top of a head and two fragments of a wreath of foliage.

A splinter has struck the Virgin on the pier, Our Lady of Reims ; it has torn the bottom of her robe. Another has wounded, above the knee, the Virgin of the Visitation. A third has grazed the lower lip of the Angel Gabriel, " the angel who smiles," and the expression on this delicate face, the finest and most life-like of them all, has been marred. Opposite to it, the scene of the Presentation has been protected by the scaffolding.

In the covings, in three places the lines of foliage have been broken.

The beautiful statues over whose identification the learned dispute, which (facing the front of the contreforts) join the central porch to the other two, have had their vestments damaged : Solomon, his cloak ; the Queen of Sheba, her robe and crown.

By the front, on the right, towards the Archbishop's

palace, the mitred personage, Solomon's neighbour, believed to be Saint Sinice, has been touched in the hand and chin. We notice also several rents in the drapery (above the *soubassement*), and, farther on, holes in the arch of the last buttress.

The left front has several victims : the first of the great statues, that which holds a book, and is taken to represent St. Maur, has no longer the whole of its hair ; the third has a wound on the right foot ; St. Nicaise, opposite, between his two angels, has received several scratches ; in the middle of the lintel, St. Paul has been lightly gashed on the cheek ; in the covings one personage has the top of his skull completely removed ; another, seated, has been decapitated. All this has come from a bomb eight or ten metres in front, close to Joan of Arc.

A shell has fallen in the courtyard of the Palais de Justice, quite close still—twelve paces away, to be exact—in the alignment of the front. It has covered with splinters the return face of the last buttress and the base of the tower, up to the first stage.

We have not much trouble in discovering, in the Rue de Robert de Coucy, the shell which broke the windows of the nave. In the middle of the road, three metres from the grille, it has burst, and dug a wide ditch, which is full of water. We plunge our hands into it : the water is still tepid, heated by the burning steel splinters. And splinters are splashed as high as the arches of the buttresses. It is this shell that just now made the Cathedral tremble, insomuch that the uproar of the explosion, echoed and amplified by the powerful acoustic properties of the structure, and the noise of falling glass, iron and plaster, had been terrifying. The soil had been shaken ; the walls had trembled under the commotion, and M. Andrieux told us that, in the clock staircase, a violent gust of air drove him and his companions literally upon their knees.

We were under the illusion that our sad inventory was now ended ; for the two shells which, at the end of the same street, had badly injured the printing works of the *Eclaireur de l'Est*, had not damaged the chapels in the apse ; and, on the other side, by the Archbishop's palace, there was nothing. But we have left out one, and that one has struck the edifice.

It is only on the 9th of September that we discover it, at the north cross-bar of the transept, at the foot of the great pediment of the Annunciation, on the level of the higher gallery : it had dislodged a large block of stone (Plate 1).

The grotesque figures which ornament the truss of the gable have been struck : that which comes down astride on the edge, with a man on its back, has had half of the face carried away ; the chimera which climbs to meet it has received a bullet in the back ; one of the compartments of the flamboyant decoration above, in the front, is broken at the corners ; the bell-turret which covers St. Michael has notches in it ; other injured parts are a small column, a dripstone, a crocket, a bird, and the cross on a buttress pinnacle.

After this, perhaps too detailed, enumeration of the wounds of Notre-Dame, the reflection made by the commandant, Lieutenant-Colonel von Kiesenwetter, may appear a trifle ironic : " If your beautiful Cathedral has not really even been grazed, it is because our gunners had received, from higher authority, a formal order to respect it."[1]

The Germans have pleaded unskilfulness, accident, and errors in firing ! That they did not especially aim at the Cathedral is likely enough, for, at seven kilometres distance, such a colossus, which dominates, with its imposing mass, the whole town—" which emerges like Gibraltar from the sea, and like the Pyramids from the desert "—constitutes an objective upon which every shot would bear. But that they had taken, as they pretend, precautions to spare it, one cannot believe, and for the same reasons.

If they had the formal order to respect it—a Staff Officer assured me that he had had the note in his hand, and had read it—it cannot be said that they paid much heed to it ; for it is scarcely respecting a monument to surround and graze it with shells, after the fashion of the Japanese jugglers who stab with daggers on each side of a man's head. And one needs only to trace on a plan the spots in front, in the rear, and in the adjacent streets, which were struck, to form the impression that this is what they tried to do. I put such a sketch before the officer : he was obliged to admit the evidence.

But, let us pass on. One does not wrangle over scratches when it is a case of murder. Even if they intended to spare it on the 4th of September, they had changed their intention before the end of the month.

[1] *Courrier de la Champagne,* 6th September, 1914.

II

THE DAYS OF TRAGEDY

Pl. 9

Photos J. Serpe (Collection J. Matot)

THE CATHEDRAL ON FIRE (NORTH SIDE) (see p. 42; face p. 20)

Pl. 10

Photo J. Matot

TWO CORPSES IN THE LOWER NAVE (*see p* 47)

Photo J. Matot

ANOTHER IN THE GREAT NAVE (*see p.* 47; *face p.* 21)

CHAPTER II

THE DAYS OF TRAGEDY

DURING the occupation, the Kommandatur was installed in the Hôtel du Lion d'Or facing the Cathedral. Day and night the Place du Parvis was encumbered with troops, men and horses, war material, wagons, field-kitchens, and trains of lorries (Plate 3). And, amid this tumultuous, clamorous coming and going, there passed,—haughty, immersed in affairs,—Von Klück, de Bülow, Princes Eitel and Wilhelm, and the Crown Prince—those masters of the moment who believed themselves already to be the masters of the world. And it hurt us to see our Joan of Arc standing there lonely, lost in the middle of this German bivouac, surrounded by Prussians, as if she was their prisoner. Her sweet and grave face, which betrays so delicately through the radiance of the soul a secret anxiety of heart, seemed to reflect this humiliation. And with her eyes gazing upwards to heaven, the sword always in her hand, she personified France invaded, turning to God, fighting, praying, suffering and hoping.

And, to add to the bitterness and melancholy of this vision, the scene was displayed before the Great Front of Our Lady of Reims !

On Sunday we expected a demand for a military Mass ; but no chaplain presented himself. One saw here and there in the congregation groups of soldiers mingled discreetly with the faithful, during the Offices. In the week there had been some at the Masses in the morning and at the Stations of the Cross in the evening. Some of them made their confession, and received Holy Communion.

On Saturday, the 12th September, at nine o'clock the district representative of the Red Cross, M. J. Lambert, and M. Berque, who acted as interpreter, came to advise me that the Germans had decided to put all their wounded into the Cathedral.

In the hope that perhaps there was still time, and that one might get this decision reconsidered, since there were plenty of places where the wounded could be better accommodated than in the Cathedral, I hastened to the Lion d'Or.

Already there was electricity in the air. The senior officers were visibly preoccupied and nervous. They were agitated ; they spoke curtly. The men, keenly on the alert, seemed more rigid and stiffer than ever. Motor-cars, flanked by soldiers with fixed bayonets, came and went in a great hurry, bringing the Mayor, Dr. Langlet, then the *secrétaire-général* of the Mairie, M. Raissac, M. Rousseau, the Deputy-Mayor, and M. Eugène Gosset, President of the Chamber of Commerce.

Isolated from the rest of the world since the 4th of September, we knew nothing of what was passing outside Reims. It was only on the evening before that a vague echo of the Conclave had reached us : there was a pope ; he was called Benedict the Fifteenth ; but who was elected ?

Pl. 11

Photo Thinot

CORPSES IN THE COURTYARD (*see p.* 50; *face p.* **22**)

Pl. 12

Photo J. Matot

PUTTING THE VICTIMS OF THE 19TH SEPTEMBER, 1914, INTO COFFINS (see p. 51; face p. 23)

Since when ? It was all a mystery. Still less did we suspect the sudden turning of the French Army on the 6th ;
or the Battle of the Marne and the defeat of the Germans
on the 8th ; or the fighting which was in progress around
Reims, and was to issue that same evening in the evacuation
of the town.

It was all this which weighed upon the Kommandatur.
The Germans were preparing feverishly for their flight,
and assembling hostages as sureties. Mgr. Neveux, Bishop-
elect of Arsinoé, had been there for ten minutes, with the
vicar-general, M. Camu ; the Abbé Andrieux was to join
them later.

A notice, placarded on our walls, informed us, by order
of the Commander-in-Chief of the German Army, that
these *hostages would be hung*, and that the town would be
burnt, partially or totally, *and the inhabitants hung*, on the
smallest attempt at disorder.

My request at such a moment was not likely to fall on
sympathetic ears. The Commandant did not want to hear
anything : " No doubt there are other available places in
the town, but it is in the Cathedral that the wounded will
be placed, by superior order."

Willingly or not, one had to make up one's mind to it.
Besides, the requisitions for forage had already been made.
The vehicles were not long in arriving, and towards the end
of the afternoon a thick couch of straw, fifteen thousand
trusses, encumbered and humiliated our three naves. The
chairs had been piled up in the choir and the sanctuary.

In point of fact they had not the time to put their
wounded here. For that same evening the town was
evacuated. The advance guard of General Franchet

23

d'Esperey's Army presented itself in the suburb of Vesle while the last convoys of Germans were still filing along the road to Vitry carrying the hostages with them to cover their retreat.

On the next day, Sunday, while the population was fêting our soldiers, we believed the others to be far away ; but they were entrenching themselves quite near on the hills which dominate the plain of Reims on the north and east.

A staff colonel had said on Friday evening to his host :[1] " *To-morrow you will hear a violent cannonade. You will probably have the moral satisfaction of seeing your own troops back ; but, behind Reims, on the heights, we shall stand firm, and we shall not loosen our grip upon you.*"

They only loosened their grip upon Reims on the 5th of October, 1918, after 857 days of actual bombardment up to the evacuation (24th March, 1918)—a bombardment which claimed more than a thousand victims from among the civil population, of whom nearly three hundred were women, and at least a hundred were children.[2]

Since Monday I had been making efforts to obtain the removal of the straw. They started upon it on Wednesday,

[1] Dr. Colaneri.

[2] There are divergences in the estimates of the number of victims. They proceed from the fact that certain enumerations were made simply upon police reports which registered from day to day the number of deaths, that is of those who were killed at once. I have the complete list of them, with dates and names, up to the 14th February, 1918 ; the total is 712, of whom 256 were women, and 90 children.

But account must also be taken of the wounded who died in the hospitals, of whom there were more than two hundred in the Civil Hospital at Reims. If one takes count, first of those, and secondly of the wounded who died in the street on the Red Cross stretchers, and who do not appear in the entry registers of the hospitals, they numbered more than thirty in 1917 ; thirdly, of those who died in their homes, and whose deaths were registered direct with the registrar of deaths ; and, fourthly, of those who were removed, on certain days, to Epernay and Châlons ; one does not exaggerate in speaking of a thousand victims among the civil population.

when suddenly the order came to do nothing more ; the arrangement had been rescinded by the French military authorities.

The ruins of Malines and Louvain gave one matter for thought. A German senior officer standing on the Parvis admiring the Cathedral had let some grave words escape from his lips, which seemed as though he were expressing pity for the coming disaster. A Berlin journal, in scarcely veiled terms, had formulated the threat : it would be prudent to bethink oneself about the matter. The Germans had wished to make the Cathedral a shelter for their wounded ; why should not we make their wounded a safeguard for the Cathedral ? An army does not fire on its own wounded : at any rate one had not seen it done yet.

That same day, the 16th, in the afternoon, very conspicuously, were brought one by one from the Hôtel-Dieu to the Cathedral, on stretchers or in open carriages, a score of wounded—others were to follow the next day[1]—and it is impossible that the Germans, informed by their spies of the smallest incidents, did not learn of this transfer the same evening.

I say " their spies," for it has been said too loudly and repeated too often, with a meaning and in a tone which have rightly offended us, that Reims was " a nest of spies." That there were spies in Reims, as everywhere else, is evident. Where were they not ? That there were more there than in the centre or south is likely enough. But to

---

[1] They came from the Place Belletour (the man conveying them was killed, with one of his wounded, by a shell, while on the journey) ; from the Rue de la Université (among whom were some severely wounded), from the premises of G. H. Mumm ; from the Rue des Chapelains ; and towards the evening, several others from the Énfant Jésus. I could not ascertain if any came to us from elsewhere.

say that there were more than in Paris, more than at Nancy, more than in any other town at the front, is a falsehood.

The Germans boast of having a legion of spies in their pay ; they have given a figure equivalent to an army corps. These, like the other troops, are mobilized ; they are sent to any spot where their services are useful ; they infest the fighting zones, and it is not surprising that during the long months of siege war at the gates of Reims, one should have noticed their presence and their activity among us, as everywhere on the front from the English Channel to Switzerland, from the Baltic to the Danube.

But Reims has shown enough courage, enough coolness and fine endurance under the fire of the enemy, and she has suffered enough, to be entitled to be spared suspicions concerning the loftiness or the sensitiveness of her patriotism.

On Saturday the 12th, on the initiative of M. Alexandre Henriot, a large Red Cross flag was displayed on the north tower, by the side of the white flag which the Germans had left there. The next day, the 13th, when the French troops entered the city, the white flag was taken away, and the tricolour was hoisted.

The great Red Cross flag was already in shreds ; its size, and above all its weight, increased by the rain, offered too great a hold to the wind ; it hung down with its staff broken.

It was necessary to replace it. I succeeded, after some trouble, in finding one of more modest and practicable dimensions, at the ambulance in the Rue des Chapelains, and I attached it to the lightning conductor, with a rapidity

Pl. 13

Photo Berthelomier

THE CATHEDRAL ON FIRE (SOUTH SIDE) *(see p. 52; face p. 26)*

Pl. 14

THE FOREST (*see p.* 52; *face p.* 27)

which, owing to the infernal music of the bombardment, was somewhat feverish.

Meanwhile, with an alb and a choir boy's red cassock, M. Thinot, aided by the sacristan, had made at the sacristy another, much bigger, but the wind very quickly threw it down, like the first. Finally M. Andrieux, a little later, brought a third flag, which made a pendant to mine, and with it weathered all the storms.

So the protective ensigns of the Geneva Convention were not lacking. At one moment there were three of them ; and all the time there were two, which continued to float, long after the fire, on the ruins.

That day, the 17th, during the heavy fighting at La Pompelle and Brimont, though only three struck the Cathedral, the shells fell thick on the town ; and the insecurity of the streets, as well as the crowding of the military hospitals, where the attendants and doctors were not sufficient for the work, had not permitted the addition to this improvised ambulance of the most indispensable services : men were lying on the floor with blankets ; and that was all—a hundred or more of wounded with a German major, himself wounded in the head, a chaplain, the Abbé Prullage, curate at Stadtholm, in Westphalia, two nuns, and a deaconess. A guard of soldiers outside kept the doors.

A French major dashed in for a moment and gave some orders ; but, overwhelmed with his own work, he was unable to return, and we did not see him again.

Bread had been requisitioned, from a long distance at the end of the town, in the Faubourg Céres—but there was no one to go for it.

Towards one o'clock two soldiers brought in upon

their shoulders an enormous quarter of a horse, which they flung down in the middle of the nave. " The Grand Hotel," they said, " which had agreed to lend its stoves, has just shut, battered in by a bomb ; they did not know at what door to knock. We must do the best we can."

The Little Sisters of the Assumption were sounded on the subject, and they agreed to cook this meat. But because of the constant shelling one could only take it to them late in the afternoon ; with the result that it was the evening, and very late, before the prisoners could get their first meal.

Friday, 18*th September.*

The parochial service had not been interrupted. On consideration we had come to the conclusion that the best means of safeguarding the Cathedral, and getting it respected, was to carry on as usual.

A large linen curtain separated the naves from the transept, and I had begged for and obtained, silence during the early hours of the morning.

The Masses were hardly finished when a shell, crashing through a window on the side of the Archbishop's palace, projected into the interior blocks of stone which killed three men[1] and wounded fifteen others.[2]

In the terrifying tumult of repeated explosions on the roofs and buttresses and roundabout, panic and distressing fright ensued among the wounded men lying in the

---

[1] The gendarme Rouillac, who had barely entered, for the purpose of searching the prisoners and ascertaining that they had no arms, was crushed on the spot with two Germans. His body, taken away to the ambulance of the Rue de l'Université, was burned there the next day in the mortuary, with a dozen other corpses of soldiers which there was no time to remove during the fire. It was necessary first to save the living.

[2] Deposition of Major Pflugmacker at Berlin, 9th January, 1915. (See Report of the Ministry of War, p. 22.)

Pl. 15

THE GREAT CROSS ON FIRE (*see p. 53; face p. 28*)

Pl. 16

OUR LADY OF REIMS, QUEEN OF THE CITY *(see p. 109; face p. 29)*

Cathedral, who now believed themselves to be lost. For there was no room for mistake, and the wounded German officers—there were five of them—were under no illusion : they were aiming at the Cathedral !

Mad with terror, those who could stand wandered about as though lost, not knowing where to hide themselves. The others, lying helpless on their litters, were groaning, imploring, crying. Where could shelter be found for them ?

I could see no other practicable refuge than the tower stairs. The clock tower staircase, in view of the direction of the firing, seemed the surest. So we bundled the wounded there, as well as we could.

Those best able to do so rushed in a crowd. The others painfully dragged themselves to it, hopping, crawling on their knees, on all fours, even on their bandages—those whose legs were amputated, on their stumps. We helped the cripples, carried those unable to move by themselves, barely clothed as they were ; dragged them ; we sat them down on the naked stone, where they had no other support than the sharp edges of the stairs. And among this miserable crowd the slightest movement provoked a groan, for it was impossible to stir without knocking some aching limbs.

A second time in the evening, and also the next morning, we had to perform over again this laborious and doleful work of conveyance.

Meanwhile we mounted to the higher stages, to escape for a moment from this agonizing obsession of suffering and disaster, to breathe more easily, and to contemplate through the battlements the other disaster outside—the destruction of the town.

The Cathedral of Reims

The *sous-préfecture* was burning, with the premises of Salaire and Fourmon. Our school in the Rue de Sedan and the boarding school of St. Symphorien which had burned the previous evening were still smoking, as well as the Vieux Anglais mill and Lelarge's factory, on the other side of the boulevard.

The neighbourhood of the Hôtel de Ville and the Colbert Barracks seemed to be special marks for the shells ; although at times one was inclined to say that the German gunners were acting like insane people, and discharging all their batteries haphazard over the town.

One's ears followed the direction of the shells. One could feel them coming—sneaking, menacing ; then suddenly bursting quite close, or maybe passing with an angry whistle over our heads, to carry destruction a little farther away. With a grip of the heart we marked the places where they fell. We recorded the wound without having seen the blow : a falling wall, a roof broken in, like a soft crust beneath a furious, invisible shock ; then a jet of smoke, black, thick, heavy, which spurted upwards, enormous and powerful, as from the crater of a volcano, the noise of the explosion reaching us a long time afterwards.

We put names to each catastrophe—the street, the house —anxious to know whether, beneath the heaps of stones, there was blood or death. Then, wearied with these violent emotions, we came down, in a still sadder frame of mind, to the desolation below.

It was all around. In a lower room an invalid was dying.[1] We had not been able to take her into the crypt : she had been installed there that she might at least have

[1] Mlle. J. Lardy, daughter of the sacristan.

shelter. With the Germans' straw we had made a bed ; and by her side, and with her, we prayed.

Someone informed me that the master bell-ringer, M. Stengel, was mortally wounded, and that his grand-daughter, a child twelve years old, had been killed on Wednesday at the Six Cadrans, by a shell which had claimed thirteen victims. Yesterday's record was still worse : seventeen sick persons killed, by one shot, with two nurses, Mme. Fondier and Mlle. Germaine Gosse, at the ambulance of Mme. de Sainte-Marie ; ten men and fifteen horses, at the Place Belletour, where there was an artillery encampment ; and, this morning, at the ambulance of the Enfant Jésus, four nuns killed and five wounded !

In the afternoon I wanted to go out to visit the hospital of the Little Sisters in the Rue du Jard, which someone told me had been struck. I had hardly turned the corner of the Archbishop's Palace when a shell fell behind me, at the corner of the Entrance facing the Lion d'Or. I retraced my steps in the smoke ; and I found, stretched out on the steps of the Parvis, a man bleeding, wounded in the abdomen.

The soldiers on guard, crouching behind their knap-sacks against the door, had not seen him, blinded as they were by the dust. They helped me to carry him into the church, where the Major examined him. He was taken away in the evening at the point of death.

Some of the wounded had been injured again, several of them by stones which had fallen upon them, others by pieces of twisted lead torn from the windows, from which their heads were bleeding. As a number of them were

Catholics, it was necessary to give them Extreme Unction ; and in this we were helped by the Abbé Schemberg, who had just come in.

It was at this moment that the Major, dismayed by the persistence of the savage bombardment, begged us to take steps to get an envoy sent to the German lines, to tell the Vandals, his brothers, that they were shooting on their own soldiers.

But how was he to get there ? And what would be the use ? They knew only too well what they were doing. It was not their own people that they wished to hit : it was the Cathedral. But rather than miss it they killed Germans : their wounded did not protect it. The Major admitted the evidence. He recognized our impotence and his own.

He had written a note of which we took a copy. It is as follows :—

" I ask to be sent as envoy, in order to inform the German Army that there are two hundred wounded[1] in the Cathedral, which is exposed to the most violent fire (*allerheftigsten*) of the artillery. I hope by this means to put a stop to the destruction of the splendid Cathedral, and a stop also to the destruction of the town.[2]

DR. PFLÜGMACKER."

[1] This figure of 200 wounded has always appeared to us to be exaggerated. The Major in his official deposition speaks only of 150. In default of a proper enumeration, M. Thinot and I wanted to give a round figure so as not to contradict ourselves when strangers and journalists interrogated us ; and we had estimated that there were not more than " une centaine."

[2] " Ich bitte als Parlementär abgesicht zu verden um dem deutschen Heeren mitteilen zu Können das 200 deutsche Verwundete in der Kathedrale liegen und dieser im allerheftigsten artillerie Feuer liegt.

" Ich hoffe, damit eine weitere Zerstörung der herrlichen Kathedrale zu verhindern und eine weitere Zerstörung der Stadt.

DR. PFLÜGMACKER."

Our wounded were, for the second time, in the shelter of the tower stairs ; M. Thinot and I had returned to the Chapel of the Blessed Sacrament to say our office. And, at each page, under the influence of the surrounding circumstances, the old words of the Book became illuminated ; they stood out in relief ; they appeared to us as though there were new, so specially adapted were they to what was actually happening.

" God, the heathens are come into Your inheritance, they have defiled Your holy temple. . . . They have poured out their blood as water ; they have killed Your servants, and there are none left to bury them. Will Your anger, Lord, endure to the end ?

" Remember not our former iniquities. Let Your mercies come quickly, for we are brought very low.

" Help us, O God, for the glory of Your name.

" Avenge the blood of Your servants which has been poured out. . . . Let the sighing of the prisoner come before You. . . .

" We are Your people, help us ! Do not tarry, for the enemy have lifted up their heads. . . . They have taken evil counsel against Your people, and have said : Come let us cut them off from among the nations, that they may be remembered no more.

" Tarry not, O Lord, but deliver us."[1]

[1] *Deus venerunt gentes in haereditatem tuam et polluerant templum sanctum tuum. . . . Effuderunt sanguinem tanquam aquam ; posuerunt morticina servorum tuorum et non erat qui sepeliret. . . . Usquequo, Domine, irasceris in finem ?*

Ne memineris iniquitatum nostrarum antiquarum.

Cito anticipent nos misericordiae tuae, quia pauperes facti sumus nimis.

Adjuva nos, Deus, propter gloriam nominis tui.

Ultio sanguinis servorum tuorum qui effusus est . . . introeat in conspectu tuo gemitus compeditorum ! . . .

Nos autem populus tuus, adjuva nos ! Ne taceas, quoniam inimici extulerunt

D

Repeatedly, amid the thunder of the explosions, the heavy pillars trembled. One heard the dull noise of formidable blows striking upon the naves and broken by the astonishing elasticity of the vaulted arches ; then came the thrill of the crashing stones ; there was one which above all made such a din, a couple of paces from us, that we thought that the whole of the apse had given way.

Hurriedly I went outside to see what had happened : it was a flying buttress from the first counterfort which had just fallen on the Lady Chapel, and broken in the roof.

Scarcely had I time to ascertain this fact when suddenly into this atmosphere of cataclysm there came running towards me a tall man, with a scared look ; he drew himself up in a dramatic attitude, and, with uplifted arms, cried in a loud voice : " There is no God ! " This cry, torn, by the violence of the scandal, from a simple soul, exasperated to the point of suffering—this cry of horror and fear, which was not intended for a blasphemy, which rather breathed the energy of outraged protest, of revolt against the sacrilege—this cry, at such a moment, in this deserted street, uttered with this gesture, with those eyes shining with anger, with that convulsed face, excited commotion in my own heart.

When an ordeal goes beyond a certain point, when it exacts too much, and the shock is too violent, the badly enlightened faith of the people becomes troubled ; it wavers, it reels over : the weak are scandalized. But the

---

caput. . . . *Super populum tuum malignaverunt consilium et dixerunt : Venite et disperdamus eos de gente et non numerentur ultra.*

Ne taceas, Domine, adjuva nos. (Cf. *Off. de Feria,* VIa, Ps. 78, 80, 82, *passim.*)

Pl. 17

Photo Thinot

Photo Thinot

THE DISASTER IN THE INTERIOR: THE CHOIR AND THE NAVES
(see p. 111; face p. 34)

Pl. 18

Photo J. Matot

DÉBRIS ROUND THE PULPIT : LUSTRES THROWN DOWN, CLOTHS, VASES,
ALMS-DISHES, AND SMALL ARTICLES SCATTERED OVER THE CINDERS

(*see p.* 111; *face p.* 35)

scandal comes back as a curse upon those who have provoked it.

Saturday, the 19*th*.

It seemed to us that nothing worse could happen to
the Cathedral than had happened yesterday, and we only
apprehended having to endure it once more, and live again
hours like those of yesterday.

The night had not been too bad. The Prussian batteries
had reawakened about two o'clock, to destroy something
fresh, to perform covertly in the darkness some work of
mischief, to make some more ruins, and claim some new
victims. Then, after a while, as though wearied, they
slept again.

In the morning the parochial service was performed as
usual. The first Masses had been fairly well attended, but the
church emptied quickly. One heard, by the front, a vague
noise of footsteps, slow and heavy, partly smothered by the
straw. Short whispers mounted, from time to time, from
the bottom of the naves. The wounded, exhausted by a
wakeful night, were asleep.

The respite was not for long. With the eight o'clock
Mass the bombardment began again, violent, furious, right
on the Cathedral.

One solitary person assisted at this Mass : it was the
last. At the Gospel I said to the boy who was serving me :[1]
" Leave me. Go. Get into shelter." He answered
courageously, " I would rather remain." And he stayed
until the end.

This lasted all the morning, all the day.

[1] Charles Buffet.

35

We had to return to the Place to get bread for the wounded ; and we were waiting for a lull, in order to fetch it.

Again we put the wounded in the tower, except the officers—there were five of them—who always kept aloof. One realized that in the German Army there was a very deep and wide gulf between officers and soldiers. Crouching in the straw, behind the pillars, near the pulpit, they remained a group apart, unmoved, and displaying no interest in the others.

We had, very late, eaten a morsel of bread in the church ; then about two o'clock we retired to the Chapel of the Blessed Sacrament to pray, counting meanwhile the shells which were persistently striking upon the walls and the roofs as though they were a battering ram intended to break down the building.

.   .   .   .

The 19th of September. On that day we sing First Vespers of the Feast of the Seven Sorrows of Our Lady ! Truly, it was appropriate. The same distress which afflicted our souls poured forth in tearful lamentation from one end of the Office to the other, putting us in unison with the distress which weighed down Mary on Calvary. It was not necessary to cast aside our own misery to compassionate that of the Mother of Sorrows.

("*O vos omnes qui transitis per viam, attendite et videte !*")

" Oh, you who to-day pass along our streets, look and say if there is greater sorrow than mine ! "

That was at this moment the lament of Our Lady of Reims ; and the Psalmist lent her the tearful accents of

Pl. 19

Photo L. Gœrens

AT A DISTANCE THE CATHEDRAL APPEARS INTACT (TAKEN FROM THE
RUE LIBERGIER) *(see p. 115, face p. 36)*

Pl. 20

Photo Thinot

THE CATHEDRAL AFTER THE FIRE *(see p. 116; face p. 37)*

the Daughter of Sion with which to utter to God her prayer: " Why am I thus forsaken, O my God ? (*Quare oblitus est mei?*) For the enemy oppresses me, without respite, the whole day, so that my bones are broken beneath his blows, (*dum confringuntur ossa mea*) ; for they are many, these soldiers who work their fury upon me ; (*quoniam multi belluntur adversum me.*) They surround me like a pack of hounds : (*quoniam circumdederunt me canes multi*).

" They have brought me to such a pass that a scandalized world asks me : Where is now your God ?

" But you, O Lord (*sed tu, Domine, usque quo?*) how far will You let them go ? "

And Jeremias in the Lesson at Matins is thus moved to compassion : " See then this beautiful creation (*perfecti decoris*), the sight of which ravishes the whole world ! Its enemies have deliberated upon its fate ; gnashing their teeth they have said, (*fremuerunt dentibus et dixerunt*): ' We will leave nothing of it (*devorabimus !*) ' "

And in the psalms the supplication becomes more urgent :—

" Oh my God, our fathers in their hours of trouble put their hope in You, and You saved them. They cried to You, and they were never confounded. Then, Lord, do not refuse Your aid to me ; come to my defence ! (*ad defensionem meam conspice !*)

" Oh, you who to-day pass along our streets, look and see if there be greater sorrow than mine ! (*O vos omnes qui transitis per viam : attendite et videte !*) "

The carillon rang out those lugubrious hours, as it had rung others, with the same equanimity as on feast days. It put forth as its prayer in the storm the hymn of the season. In September it should have been the *Iste Confessor* ; but, owing to the disarrangement caused by the war, the cylinders had not been changed, and since the Assumption it had continued to play the *Ave Maris Stella* —as though it wished to die saluting Our Lady.

Its clear notes fell on the air serenely like an appeasing hush from heaven upon our desolation, like an appeal inviting confidence, that eyes blinded with tears might be lifted up to God on high ; that souls overwhelmed beneath the ordeal might stand erect again and echo the *Sursum Corda*.

This angelic chant, mingling with that tempest of hell, accentuated its brutality. One had the impression of a hostile power, tenacious, stubborn, insistent, in a merciless struggle to overthrow the temple. The shells bit into the stone, broke down the walls, battered in the roofs, made havoc with statues, pinnacles, bell turrets and counter-forts. But the bruises were not deep enough, nor the wounds wide enough ; the mass of the structure was not broken ; the cannon had not succeeded in that. The monstrous howitzers had not arrived. The noble mutilated building still stood erect, more majestic than ever under the tempest. It also was stubborn, and would not perish. And then, in their stupid and sacrilegious rage, as supplement to the hurricane of iron they unchained the hurricane of fire in order to compass the destruction.

It would be about three o'clock, or a quarter-past, that we were told that smoke was coming from the scaffolding of the north tower. Without losing a minute, we rushed outside, to the Rue Robert de Coucy, to see for ourselves. There was no doubt about it ; the scaffolding was in flames about midway up, at the back of the tower, facing the Rue du Trésor.

At ordinary times the members of the fire brigade, whose devotion in these sinister days, with Adjutant Effoire at their head, was admirable, would soon have had the fire in hand ; but now there were fires in various quarters of the town ; and so hands, pumps and water were all lacking.

In the hope that perhaps we could do something M. Thinot and I tried to mount the scaffold.

Four stages at least were blazing in the middle, four circular fires, one above the other, marking probably the passage of a shell (Plate 8).

We tried to pull down the heavy beams, but unsuccessfully. We called out, but no one heard. Shells were bursting on the town at all points.

The carillon sounded the half-hour, and repeated like a knell its brief supplication : " *In manus tuas, Domine, commendo spiritum meum.*"

We thought that the scaffolding would burn, and then fall, and that that would be all ; we hoped it, at any rate. If it had not been that there was straw, and so much straw, in the Cathedral, we should not have feared a catastrophe in the interior. But a spark sufficed.

We came down to avert, if possible, the peril which threatened ; for the glass of the windows surely would break soon, and the wounded would be burned with the straw.

We betook ourselves to the task of throwing the straw outside in the yard. Some of the prisoners helped us ; M. Andrieux, who speaks German, directed the work.

Sparks were already entering by the holes in the windows. We watched them. We seized them in their flight, one by one, and stamped them out.

But outside the fire was continually increasing. It advanced and gained the façade. We felt it come. We divined its approach by the redder tints (as if suffused with blood) which flushed the windows at the Entrance.

Soon we heard a hard cracking noise : half of the Great Rose broke, and a thick smoke entered through the breach. And just at this moment a ray of sunlight, the only one we had seen during this day of fog and rain, filtered softly through the gaping wound, slowly travelled along the nave to the sanctuary, caressed the altar, remained there a moment, and then disappeared.

Man's effort proves powerless : we are defeated.

The arches are still trembling beneath the shells.

Suddenly, with a terrifying rumble, and the sound of breaking and crashing, the scaffolding falls on the Parvis, and fire-flakes flutter in eddies under the roofs.

There was not a minute to lose. Steps must be taken to save the wounded. I gave orders to collect them all under the organ and in the apse.

I can see again that piteous mobilization of sick, maimed, impotent, limbless men, who interrogated us with eyes big with fear, and hastened painfully, moaning, crying, bleeding, across the north transept. Some we carried, others we dragged ; those who could not move we lifted on a stretcher.

Once we had got these men away from the field of straw and far from the threatened naves, I deemed it prudent to place the Blessed Sacrament in safety. Without saying anything, I carried It—in four ciboria—to the Convent of the Nuns of the Adoration Réparatrice, whence, half an hour later, the Prioress had to carry It away still further, because her convent was burning.

I had scarce re-entered the Cathedral when I saw, with a feeling of stupor, the glimmer of fire in the apse, and the windows resplendent with flames.

Without being able to explain to myself how it came, without giving myself the time to reflect on it, I had a very distinct sensation of irremediable catastrophe : the fire had caught the woodwork in the roof ; all was lost !

I cried out at once to M. Andrieux and M. Thinot and to M. Divoir, who had just arrived : " Let us save the Treasure ! "

While they forced the doors of cupboards I ran outside to find hands to help. Several excellent workmen, whose names I wish I knew, responded to my appeal, and the whole of the Treasure—the Holy Phial, the Chalice of St. Rémi, the Reliquary of the Holy Thorn, old shrines dating back to the Middle Ages, the Vessel of St. Ursula, the relics of St. John Baptist de la Salle, the Consecration ornaments, were all rapidly conveyed into a place of safety.

Already the flames are devouring the chevet ; they scale up " the steeple of the angel " ; they spread over the great roofs ; everywhere they are licking the lead plates of the roof which, little by little, vanishes and discloses the bare " forest "—that enormous mass of woodwork whose frame stands out, across the interlacing galleries, like a prodigious skeleton of fire.

We hear the bells falling.

Little rivulets of lead run in the channels and are spat

out through the gargoyles ; they drip down in heavy tears, which are flattened on the floors of the lower stages and fly back in fine dust ; and these splashings, mixed with the sparks which were flying all around, in the smoke, in the flame-lit air, prick us on the face and hands as we traverse the courtyard with our precious burdens.

I estimate that the interval between our ascent into the scaffolding and the moment when the fire blazed out on all sides was scarcely more than an hour.

That fire had broken out in several places, common sense, in default of other proof, left us no room for doubt. The Cathedral was burning at both ends, though the middle was still intact ;—and it was not the scaffolding which had set light to the roofs.

Besides, witnesses are not lacking.[1] They observed from quite different points, and with the aid of field-glasses. They saw a fresh shell fall upon the chevet ; then two others upon the roof of the central nave, one towards the north and the other to the south. They separately noted their observations ; and those observations agree. So there had been, counting the scaffolding, four distinct fires. Finally, we have the brutal proof, the undeniable documentary evidence of photographs, which proves the fact beyond the possibility of contradiction.

And they cannot, this time, cloak their evil deed under an equivocation, by talking of accident. They cannot entrench themselves behind fatality. For, instead of stopping, surprised and shamed, when they saw the flaming

---

[1] A whole group of officers ; a religious, Fr. Etienne ; three medical men, Doctors Gerbet (of Rouen), Raoult (of Vernon), and Legrand ; a magistrate, M. Bauduin de Bunier ; the police commissaire, M. Speneux ; M. Poirier, of the firm of Pommery ; M. Huart, the guardian of the museum ; and others.

scaffold, they offended again ; they struck afresh—once, twice, three times, as one strikes—rather, as they strike— a wounded man on the battle-field to finish him off.

The Cathedral was bombarded and fired by batteries of the Seventh Army, under the command of General Josias von Heeringen.

.   .   .   .

Concerning the incident which follows I would prefer to say nothing, but since it has been spoken of, since it is spoken of still, and not always accurately, here it is :—

I had accompanied the men who were transporting the Treasure, to see where they put it, how they had installed it, and if it was sheltered from fire and shells, and I regained the church slowly, without knowing much what I should do there. I was heart-broken, overwhelmed with grief and a sense of impotence, as I walked past the old Archbishop's Palace, now burning, and the convent by its side, which was in flames, along streets, throughout the length of which the flames were now licking—an entire quarter behind the burning Cathedral turning into an immense brasier.[1]

One heard only the crackling and the roaring of the flames, like the noise of a tempest, above, below, before, behind, far away, everywhere. I had the impression of being alone ; in the Rue du Cloître, no one : no one either in the Rue Robert de Coucy. But, walking on, I suddenly perceived, barring the Rue du Préau, facing the small

[1] According to the official report of the highway authority, the ravages of the fire on the 18th and 19th of September covered over the entire town a surface of fourteen hectares (some thirty-five acres), of which eight hectares were burned in one unbroken space—" the Woollen Quarter "—behind the Cathedral.

43

Entrance, some soldiers lined up, kneeling, their rifles raised.

At first I did not realize what was happening. But the door opened, and I saw, massed in the lobby, the wounded !

I understood then. They had not come out ; they were not allowed to come out. Behind them the fire ; before them the rifles !

I cried to the sergeant : " Wretched man, what are you going to do ? "

" We have our orders."

" It is impossible," I said, " there is a mistake. What has now occurred was not foreseen. They must come out. You will not fire upon unarmed wounded men, even if they are Germans ! On the battle-field it is war ; but here it would be a crime."

" We are obliged to do it. Those are our orders."

For four or five minutes we discussed the matter, amid the noise of the fire and the bombardment, and as they would not give way, and as a mob had already gathered round the soldiers to excite them, I said, placing myself before the door : " Very well ; you will commence with me."

To fire upon a prisoner who tries to escape is an inexorable order. But that was not the case here. There was no attempt at escape ; the soldiers misunderstood, if not the principle of the order, at any rate its immediate application. Of that I am certain.

The situation, for a simple sergeant, was a delicate one. An order cannot be discussed. He did not dare to bend it to the circumstances. He had not the time to refer to

Pl. 21

Photo Sainsaulieu

VIEW OF THE NORTH TOWER (*p.* 116)
TWO BELL-TURRETS, WITH PINNACLES DESTROYED, COLUMNS BROKEN,
AND STATUES BURNED AND EATEN AWAY (*see p.* 119; *face p.* 44)

Pl. 22

Photo Thinot

AFTER THE FIRE (NORTH SIDE)

A RUBBISH-HEAP AT THE FOOT OF THE TOWER (see p. 116; face p. 45)

his superior officers. Yet he had to make up his mind, and at once ; for we did not know what was happening in the Cathedral, and we believed the danger to be imminent.

I interposed to suggest a way out of the difficulty, without compromising anybody. But I had to parley still further before we reached an agreement.

On the formal promise that no one would attempt to escape (for I answered for them all) we were to conduct the wounded under escort to the Hôtel de Ville, there to hand them over to the military authorities. The engagement was made through one of the German officers who spoke French, and at last the rifles were lowered.

Then, preceded by myself, and surrounded by the soldiers, the pitiable cortège set forth. Several of them had scraped up brooms and sticks and boards to serve them as crutches ; some were carried on stretchers.

But meanwhile the crowd had increased. The sight, in such an environment, illumined by the burning Cathedral, exasperated these people. They saw in these wounded men simply Germans—nay, Germany herself, the accursed Germany, suddenly appearing before their eyes as though caught in the very act of the crime ; and, vehemently and with clenched fists they cried out their hate and scorn, demanding vengeance and death.

Among the most excited were some who bore a singular resemblance to the street loungers, the careless *flâneurs* who, a week before, had been joking with the Germans in public, and whose attitude had disgusted us.

Vainly I appealed, not to their Christian charity—they would not have understood me—but to their good sense,

45

to those springs of generosity and loyalty which vibrate so easily in the heart of the people ; to their patriotism, explaining that the abominable crime which Germany had just committed would arouse to-morrow the indignation of the whole world, and that France would expose herself to a like reprobation if she replied by an act of cowardice, by another crime ; vainly I told them that I was more deeply hurt, more indignant, than any of them—and that in protecting the wounded I was caring for the honour of my country : it had no effect.

M. Thinot had rejoined me, and after M. Andrieux. I saw and heard them, in other groups, trying, like myself, and with no more success, to appease this storm, which minute by minute gathered force, with each fresh accession of people.

We understood only too well the fury of that crowd. Its anger, truly, was justified, in a certain fashion and in a certain measure. It had excuses ; the moment was a tragical one ; heads were turned, nerves were strained, by the terrible emotions of that day, by the horror of the disaster, by the acute bitter suffering, which had suddenly bitten at the heart of this people at the sight of the Cathedral in its death-agony. They loved it so much, though without knowing why ; they were so proud of it.

A crowd is impulsive ; it does not reason, it will not listen ; it is brutal, without pity. It acts, it strikes, and then afterwards is moved to pity, even to tears, when the mischief is done.

We had not gained the Courtyard of the Chapter House when we were brought to a complete standstill. A captain of dragoons rode by ; I begged him to intervene.

Pl. 23

Photo Doucet

THE PORCH OF THE NORTH TOWER
THE QUEEN OF SABA AT THE POINT OF THE COUNTERFORT ON THE RIGHT
(see p. 117; face p. 46)

Pl. 24

THE QUEEN OF SABA: BEFORE AND AFTER *(see p. 117; face p. 47)*

" You will never," he said, " reach the Hôtel de Ville ; you must give it up."

And he undertook the responsibility of getting the Co-operative Printing Works opened, so that the Germans might be shut up there.

I believed that they had all been saved that evening. But the next day, on entering the Cathedral, where the débris of the fire was still smoking, we found three of them, burned on the spot, their limbs convulsed with pain, and on their faces the fixed expression of a supreme vision of fear and anguish (Plate 10). One of them in particular I can see now ; with great trouble the Abbé Andrieux and I had placed him on a stretcher. In order to answer the desperate appeal of another, we had handed him over to the care of two Germans, who carried him away : surprised, doubtless by the fire, they had left him. Yet they had only four steps to take.

I was not a witness of what passed on the other side, on the Parvis ; so I can say nothing of that. It has been said, and repeated widely, that the wounded were evacuated by the Great Entrance. So it has been written in the newspapers, in the reviews, and even in books. Photographs, so easily " faked," and fantastic pictures, have represented the scene. *The truth is that not one wounded man left by the Great Entrance*, because the fire prevented access to it on each side : outside, before the two doors which, if necessary, could have been made to open, and which ended by burning, the wood of the scaffolding was being consumed as in an infernal brasier ; inside, the straw was flaming, and precisely against these same two doors more violently than anywhere else, because there was there a stack of straw in reserve which had not been spread out. Besides, had it been possible, there was no one here to undertake a rescue as dangerous as it was useless, since the fire left the other door on the Rue Robert de Coucy free, and the wounded were massed under the great organ in the transept.

It is quite natural that the idea of seeking shelter in the yard should have occurred to several of them ; for during these three days, under the surveillance of soldiers, this courtyard had been used by the ambulance as a necessary annexe. That some, belated in the nave, and surprised by the firing of the straw, had been forced to seek refuge there is certain, since we found several of them there some days later under the ruins of burnt outhouses, and some more in April, when the yard was cleared out. These, being in the midst of the furnace, and burned to the bones, had no longer a human form.

The Report on the bombardment of the Cathedral published in Berlin in 1915, under the auspices of the Ministry of War,[1] suggests that the German wounded were massacred in the courtyard of the Archbishop's Palace, by the troops and the crowd, and in such fashion that " scarcely any of them were saved."

The simple enormity of this accusation is sufficient to do justice to it. It violates common sense. Is it likely that such a scene, of which the crowd would have been not only witness, but in which it would have taken an active part, could have taken place without our learning of it next day, without the whole town knowing, without

---

[1] *Die Beschiessung der Kathedrale von Reims.* Kriegsministerium, Berlin, 1915.

48

public opinion being moved,[1] without any traces subsisting, without corpses being there to witness to it ?

Now, it is a matter of public notoriety in Reims that, save for the victims of the fire, " the German wounded were saved." No one denies that, in the Rue Libergier, the Rue Trudaine, and at the approaches of the Parvis, the crowd had been in effervescence, uttering cries, abuse and threats. We have been told so at any rate. But on that side the exasperated crowd was held at a distance by the fire, and was not in contact with the Germans. Those whom it saw at close quarters were those who were conducted later, and not without trouble, with the Chaplain, from the buildings of the old Seminary, to the new museum in the Rue Chanzy.

That there had been something more than curses is certain ; there had been rifle shots, fired by isolated soldiers, who were beside themselves—by impulsive men maddened by catastrophes and ceasing to reason : that again has been told to me. It was spoken of without any mystery on the next and the following days. But one knew what there was in all this by the results. The most hot-headed of those infuriated creatures of the evening before were calmed the next day, and were congratulating themselves that the excitement had passed without cause for deploring the addition of shame to our misfortune.

There was, besides the unfortunates who perished in the fire, one killed whose body we found on Sunday morning

---

[1] The universal opinion was summed up in an observation made to me two days later by a well-known Freemason, an ex-Venerable of the Lodge, and a militant anti-clerical, who accosted me in the street, and said : " You have prevented a misfortune. If they had been killed we should not have been proud of it to-day. You have done well." And he added, offering me his hand : " But it is only a priest who could have done it." I record the conversation for its documentary value.

E

in the yard ; and it was sad enough that this should have happened. M. Thinot, who photographed everything with a care for precision and completeness which seemed to us excessive, photographed this body also (Plate 11) ; had there been others he would have photographed them all.

The depositions collated at Berlin in January, 1915, speak of point-blank firing, of massacres, of torrents of blood, of savage scenes which the courtyard had witnessed that evening.

Having seen nothing of this myself I cannot offer any direct or personal evidence, or say anything more than I have been told, but I can affirm that the appearance of the places in question the next morning did not in the least correspond with these sanguinary pictures. One can only suppose that " in this Hell " as they phrase it—and in truth, with the fire and the shouts and the shooting, it was one —eyes enlarged by fear saw more horrors than there were in fact to see.[1]

On the night of the 19th–20th the chaplain of the 52nd Division, M. Debeauvais, helped by stretcher-bearers and soldiers, attended to the transfer of those who had been saved from the Cathedral. He conducted them to the ambulances of the Rue Martin-Peller, whence they were afterwards evacuated to the rear, by the Muizon railway station. And the chaplain of the 3rd Ambulance of the 52nd Division, who received them, has written me that

[1] The principal witness for the prosecution in this affair is the Chaplain Prullage, and he gives evidence as an eye-witness (see Annex to the Report V, p. 23). Now, after having declared that he was among those who sought refuge in the sheds in the yard, and who did not go back into the Cathedral (p. 29), he relates in detail, not only all that occurred inside, but also the scenes in the Rue de Préau and in the Cour du Chapitre, on the other side. He speaks, assuredly, of more than his eyes can have seen ; and this fact, it must be admitted, does not give weight to his deposition.

Pl. 25

Photo Sainsaulieu

THE ANGEL OF SAINT NICAISE DECAPITATED (THE SMILE OF REIMS)
(see p. 117; face p. 50)

Pl. 26

Photo Thinot

THE STATUES OF THE PORCH OF THE NORTH TOWER (see p. 117; face p. 51)

they numbered 124. Now, if one adds to them, first, the victims of the fire (Plate 12), then the four or five (at least) whom the Germans themselves had killed by their bombardment,[1] one gets very near to the round figure of one hundred and fifty given by the Major. What, then, are we to think of that phrase in the official Report : " Scarcely any of them were saved " (p. 11) ?[2]

The two nuns and the Protestant nurse, Alvine Ehlert, had succeeded on Saturday evening in reaching first the house of M. Andrieux, then the surgery of Dr. Lardenois and the Roederer cellars. M. Debeauvais went to seek them on Monday, to take them back with the others, to the Rue Martin-Peller. Sister Alvine Ehlert, who as a nurse, had been right through the Balkan campaign in 1912, declared, during the journey, that she had seen " horrible " things there, but that " they were nothing by the side of the things she had seen in this war." The official reports of the atrocities committed by the Germans in Belgium, in Alsace and in France explain, illustrate and justify her evidence.

The sight of the town on fire, on the evening of this sinister 19th of September, defies description. When misfortune attains to such proportions neither pen nor pencil is equal to the task. One suffers in truth " beyond what one can tell." It seems as though the heart strings are wrenched, as if they would break ; and to this mental anguish there is added a dull sensation of indescribable lassitude.

Nevertheless, eyes and thoughts tear themselves from

[1] Cf. pp. 28, 32.
[2] Sister Alvine Ehlert, whose deposition figures in the Report (p. 20), declared that according to what she heard when she rejoined the others, " *some* of the wounded were killed."

these spectacles of woe, and instinctively return to the Cathedral. And the unfortunates whom the scourge chases, street by street, from their homes, who wander distracted and weeping through the night, seeking a resting-place and shelter, forget for a moment their distress as they pass by it ; they stop and contemplate it a long while, and find more burning and bitter tears with which to compassionate its agony.

Up above, in fact, the work of death is being accomplished. A thick smoke, driven back by a north-west wind, extends as far as St. Rémi's church. The Angel turret has resisted for a long time. We see it oscillate as if it were hesitating and seeking a place in which to lie down to die ; then it collapses, bends over, and suddenly falls, towards the Palace of the Archbishops.

The Carillon with the roofs has disappeared. And in the immense void the eye persists in searching across the eddy of fire for the familiar lines, the accustomed forms of the structure. The towers above this empty terrace seem to be inordinately elongated.

At the extremities of the transept the gables remain standing. Nothing now sustains them. They stand out against the sky, slender and frail, in a dizzy poise. It seemed as though a breath would throw them down, as if a child's hand could topple them over.

Without doubt the Guardian Angels of Our Lady's Cathedral watched over those two great panels of stone which recall the most glorious scenes in the life of Mary : the sacred hour when God condescended to her, in the ineffable smile of the Annunciation ; the radiant hour when she mounted to God in the apotheosis of her Assumption.

52

Pl. 27

Photo Sainsaulieu

THE COVINGS OF THE LEFT PORCH (THE IRON SUPPORTS ABOVE THE CARIATIDE,
ON THE LEFT, BELONGED TO THE RHINOCEROS' MOUTH GARGOYLE AT
THE FOOT OF THE STATUE OF DAVID PLAYING THE HARP:

(See Plate 29) (see p. 117; face p. 52)

Pl. 28

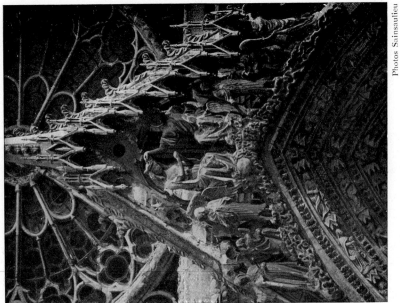

THE CORONATION OF OUR LADY (see p. 118; face p. 53)

THE CRUCIFIXION (see p. 117)

The Days of Tragedy

That evening a flying officer, Commandant Capitrel, while returning to his station, flew over the Cathedral, going from north to south, at a height of two thousand metres,[1] and he saw a spectacle which no one else could see.

While from below our eyes could no longer discover anything, above, on the roofs, in the timbers of the arches, a dull fire—a silent furnace, without flames or smoke, was glowing ; and this furnace, its contours clearly outlined by the nave and the transept, formed, stretched over the city, an immense fiery cross, the Cross of the Redemption : disaster, spread out before the face of Heaven, moulded itself into the symbol of hope.[2]

Later, when from the towers to the chevet the holocaust was consummated, we saw for a long time, burning and shining in the darkness, an enormous ember which seemed to be suspended in mid-air. It was the " Sagittaire "—a massive block of mahogany, circled with iron and fixed in the gable, which was burning.

It was there, between earth and sky, at the extreme point of the gable of the Assumption, that the fire threw into the night its final gleam.

---

[1] Commandant Capitrel had already passed over some hours before, during the fire, and he also noted that the apse had caught fire before the great roof of the nave ; he saw the Cathedral " burning at both ends." He noted that the Place du Parvis was deserted.

[2] " The spectacle was grand and terrifying," writes the commandant. " It has fallen to my lot while flying to witness impressive sights—the burning of Dinant, at dawn on the 20th of August, as well as of the villages and small towns of the Sambre ; I had contemplated, in the twilight of the 13th of September, the fires which lit up the battlefields from the Oise to the Argonne, whose acrid smoke I had breathed at a height of 2500 metres ; their tragic horror had made me tremble with anger ; but not one of these spectacles had moved me to such grief as this enormous fiery cross, in a flaming aureole—cross of martyrdom and of hope, which, invisible from below, offered itself on that evening alone to Heaven."

III

THEIR FALSEHOODS

CHAPTER III

THEIR FALSEHOODS

THEY used the Lie as a weapon of war, an element in the national defence. They could say with the pagan potentates whom Isaias castigated in his chapter of Curses : " We have entered into a league with death, and we have made a covenant with hell. When the overflowing scourge shall pass through, it shall not come upon us : for we have placed our hope in lies, and by falsehood we are protected."[1] They lied as men have never lied before. They have lied everywhere, on every subject, and with a self-possession and ease which imposed upon the whole world. They gloried in it. " They say that we lie. Yes, we do. We will go on lying, until times are better, and then we'll stop."[2] Where and when, indeed, one asks, have they not lied ?

They lied to their own people, to their own soldiers. They misled opinion in neutral countries. They deceived the Pope. They would have deceived God had they been able, when they coupled their *Gott mit uns !* to their iniquities.

Frederick the Second's great friend, Voltaire, the apologist of the Lie, did not, so far as this people is concerned, waste his time. Long ago, Julius Cæsar knew them

---

[1] Isaias xxviii. 15.   [2] Quoted by the *Strassburger Post*.

as " perfidious and liars " ; and a historian of the first century declared that they had " lying in their blood."[1]

According to them, it was we who provoked them by bombarding Nuremburg ![2] If they invaded Belgium, it was because, before them, we had violated the Belgian frontier ![3] If they are hard with our prisoners, it is because we maltreated theirs ! If they poisoned us with their asphyxiating gas, they did it in spite of their wishes, because for a long time we had done the same to them ![4] If they sometimes torpedoed hospital ships, they were forced to do it, because those boats carried combatants !

At Louvain, at Malines, at a score of other places, when they felt the desire to sack a town, they said that the civil population had fired upon them. At Reims they pretended that we had turned the Cathedral into a fortress—troops within, cannon above, machine-guns, military posts, an ammunition depôt, light signals ; and I know not what else !

[1] *Perfidia et simulatione usi Germani* (Cæsar, *Bell. Gall.*, IV, 13). *Natum mendacio genus*, Velleius Paterculus. (Quoted by Zeller in *Les Origines de l'Allemagne*, I, 204.)

[2] The German Ambassador, Herr de Schoen, declared, on the 3rd August, 1914, to his Government, in an official despatch, that French aviators, violating the frontier, had destroyed the rails between Carlsruhe and Nuremburg, and that this fact had precipitated the war ; the Chancellor affirmed it the next day in the Reichstag. And we had to wait until the 3rd of April, 1916, to obtain the denial which the military command of Nuremburg was forced to give, because nothing like what was alleged had taken place. (See L. Barthou, *Discours à Genève*, 26th July, 1916.)

[3] All the Governments concerned have published diplomatic documents relative to this grave question of responsibility for the war. But whereas our Yellow Book contains 159 documents, the British Blue Book 160, the Belgian Grey Book 83, and the Russian Orange Book 76, one is at least surprised to find that the German White Book has produced only 28. And since all these documents necessarily hang together, and reply to one another, are explained and controlled the one by the others, one is forced to the conclusion that there has been, on the part of Germany, reticence and dissimulation, adroit selections and interested suppressions.

[4] Reply of Germany to the International Red Cross Committee, September, 1918.

58

This Reims lie would be a particularly cynical one, if the destruction of the Cathedral had been decided upon in advance. Was there premeditation?

If absolute proofs are lacking, we have at least presumptions to go upon in thinking that there was premeditation.

At what moment, and in what circumstances, did they condemn it? What motive impelled them? Only those who determined on the crime could tell us; and as yet they have not boasted of it. They have given the pretext; but the reason?

How can one believe that an obscure battery commander—not even a superior officer—could have taken the initiative in such an act, without being openly cashiered and disavowed the very next day, if his act had been contrary to the Master's wish? The German Government would not have hesitated to sacrifice a man, rather than shoulder that responsibility before the world and before history.

But it is a fact that neither diplomatic quarters nor the Press, which had been busy with the lie, have ever talked of blame or disavowal.

Was the idea a sudden conception in the German brain? A saying attributed to J. Görres in 1814, which demanded the destruction " of that basilica of Reims, in which Clovis was consecrated," has been quoted on all sides. But its authenticity has been contested.[1]

There has also been recalled a phrase from Heine—a prediction, perhaps, rather than a threat. It is from his book on Germany, published in 1834. It runs:

[1] Cf. *German Reply to the French Attacks*, by Prof. A. J. Rosenberg, p. 107.

The Cathedral of Reims

" The Christian civilization will disappear from Germany, and the ferocity of the ancient Germans will break out anew. . . . Then—and that day, alas ! will come—the old warlike divinities will rise from their fabulous tombs ; they will wipe from their eyes the dust of centuries. Thor will arm himself with his gigantic hammer, and *will destroy the Gothic Cathedrals !* "[1]

[1] Thor, the son of Wotan (or Odin), is one of those gods of the sanguinary religion of ancient Germany whom Charlemagne believed he had vanquished. He is the un- pitying god of combats, the god of force, the personification of such a war as the Germans have conceived and waged.

The Christian Faith, which came late among them, was superimposed upon the myths of Germany. The instinct of the race, with its strange mixture of brutality and dreaminess, has persisted, held in check and attenuated by civilization, but not destroyed. The German brain has never been completely cleansed ; an old core of pagan atavism remains.

Among other works of the same kind, the curious study by M. F. Brenier, in the May–June, 1915, number of the *Revue Antimaçonnique,* on the survival of Odinism in Germany, throws light upon this enigma of the " old German god, *Deutscher alte Gott,*" who is not the God of the Gospel. And the strange echo which this German god poetry has fanned in the German soul of the twentieth century, the success which they have made of it, the popularity which it has enjoyed, all counts as an avowal.

" You have, then, a God whom we do not know ? "

" Yes, and if you do not know him we will tell you. The God who speaks through our cannon, who destroys your fortresses, who roars in the heavens with our airships, the God of those swords of ours which have filled you with dismay, he it is who, through the centuries, has watched over Germany—the Wotan of our fathers, he and no other. It was he of whom Walther sang. It was he in whose strength Luther fought, who gave to our land Lessing and Kant and Goethe. All that is from him, the God whom we supplicate to-day—the Holy Spirit of Germany ! " (Quoted by M. E. Prüm, leader of the Catholic party of Luxembourg, in his charge against the Catholics of Germany.)

Had not Neitzsche already spoken in the same sense ? " You have heard of men who said : Blessed are the peacemakers ! But I say to you : Blessed are those who make war, for they shall be called if not the children of Jehovah, at any rate *the children of Odin,* who is greater than Jehovah." (Quoted from *Les Études,* August, 1905, p. 222.)

I take from *The Refutation of French Attacks,* of Professor Rosenberg, this avowal : " There exists in Germany a specific Catholic religious culture and a specific non- Catholic religious culture, which latter is again divided into special religious cultures. *The cult of Wotan* (if one may attribute to it the quality of a religious culture) is one of the last and most recent of these manifestations " (p. 111).

60

Pl. 29

Photo Doucet

DAVID PLAYING THE HARP; FANTASTIC GARGOYLE
(SUBJECTS DESTROYED BY THE FIRE) (*see p* 118; *face p.* 60)

Pl. 30

Photo Thinot

THE GALLERY OF THE "GLORIA" (*see p.* 118; *face p.* 61)

They have pretended that this quotation does not apply, because it refers to their own cathedrals, not to ours.

Was it thanks to their kindness that they did not burn down Reims Cathedral in 1814 ? Was it not rather that the Russians and the British prevented them ? And did they not, in 1870, bombard the Cathedral of Strasbourg,[1] as Frederick the Second, in 1757, had bombarded the Cathedral of Prague ?

Have they not had the cynicism to bestow upon Werder, the wretched hero of Strasbourg, that same title of honorary member[2] of the University with which Koenigsmarck, in his time, had already been gratified, for having destroyed the Parthenon ?

But without exhuming from the dust of libraries far-off provocations, we have echoes of German thought more recent.

Under date of the 5th of September, 1914, a Berlin journal, the *Berliner Tageblatt*, returned to the same idea :

---

[1] " The Germans on the 15th of August opened fire upon Strasbourg. On the night of the 23rd, wishing to force a quick decision, Werder began the bombardment.

" Then one sees this astonishing thing, unknown since barbarian times : it is neither against the ramparts nor the garrison that the shells are hurled, but upon the innocent town, upon the women, the children, the old men, upon the precious museums, the libraries, the churches, the temples, upon the priceless cathedral, the legacy and jewel of the ages !

" Fire at the Museum ! Fire at the Arsenal ! Fire at the Library ; at the Temple Neuf, at the Palais de Justice ! The Broglie and the Hôtel de Ville are also included. And upon this scarlet sheet the cathedral, riddled with shells, burns in its turn, and flames over all its immense roof of metal." (Cf. P. and V. Margueritte, *Histoire de la Guerre*, 1870–71.)

[2] The *Frankfort Gazette* of the 6th June, 1915, declares that the distinction was not awarded on this account, but was given as a recognition for having preserved Germany from invasion. It nevertheless remains true that the crime of Strasbourg was no obstacle in the way of conferring the honour.

"The eastern group of our armies of France has already passed the second line of defensive forts except Reims, *whose royal splendour*, going back to the time of the white lilies, *will not fail to roll in the dust very soon*, beneath the blows of our 420 guns."[1]

It is true that about the same time the *Frankfort Gazette* struck a different note.

" Let us," it wrote, " respect the French Cathedrals, that of Reims in particular, which is one of the most beautiful basilicas in the world. Since the Middle Ages it has been specially dear to Germans, for the Master of Bamberg got his inspiration for several of his faces from the statues on its porticoes.

" The Cathedrals of Laon, Rouen, Amiens, and Beauvais are also masterpieces of Gothic art. All these cities are at this moment occupied by the Germans. We will regard those grand churches with veneration, and we will respect them, as our fathers did in 1870."[2] Are there, then, two schools, a dual current of opinion, or rather two successive states—the second that of an enemy who repents of his first ideas ? " We occupy ; we are conquerors ; those Cathedrals are ours ; let us guard them."

But after their defeat at the Marne, when disillusion has come and all hope of maintaining themselves in Champagne has gone ; when the prey escapes them, they turn upon it in fury, and crush it : " As we cannot have it, no one shall ! "

On the morrow of the battle, eight or ten days before

[1] Cf. *Berliner Tageblatt* of the 5th September, 1914, No. 208.

[2] *Frankfort Gazette*, 8th September, 1914. Quoted in the *Temps* of the 21st September, 1914.

Pl. 31

Photo Thinot

THE GREAT NAVE EMPTY (see p. 120; face p. 62)

Pl. 32

Photo Thinot

A CALCINATED PILLAR (GREAT NAVE) (see p. 121; face p. 63)

the event, Prussian soldiers spoke of it among themselves on the Parvis; postcards representing the catastrophe already—the Cathedral in flames—were seen in the hands of several; and one officer, of such high rank that the others bowed very low before him, made there a transparent allusion in a tone which seemed rather to deplore and compassionate. Whilst he was accompanying, as far as the door of the hotel, a Red Cross nurse who asked help from him for her ambulance, he said to her, waving his hand towards the Cathedral: " It is beautiful, is it not? . . . We shall not preserve it."[1]

On Friday the 11th, in the Rue du Cloître, a captain, his arm stretched out towards the Cathedral, uttered aloud to his men, in German, this reflection: " The French are proud of it. We will destroy it."

Another officer, who lodged under the very shadow of the Cathedral, said, by way of farewell to his host, on the doorstep, also with an attitude of commiseration: " Superb Cathedral! . . . Poor Cathedral! "

Two non-commissioned officers, in a café in the Rue Saint Jacques, said: " If we are obliged to retreat, and evacuate Reims, we will destroy the Cathedral."[2]

Doubtless these are only scraps of conversation caught by the way, phrases heard in the street, and one must not give them an importance which perhaps does not attach to them; but there is no smoke without fire. How can one explain these various intimations, these menaces formulated in the Press, these reflections, these hints, if there had not been something in the air?

[1] Madame Comte.

[2] The conversation took place before several persons. M. Dramas, of the *Eclaireur de l'Est*, himself heard it.

Did not Prince August Wilhelm tell the municipality : " To destroy your Cathedral would be a crime that I do not wish to commit, and I will put my wounded there to preserve it ? " Preserve it from what ? He believed it was threatened. By whom ?

Attempts have been made to explain all these excesses, all these useless devastations, by a brutal awakening, beneath the Germanic culture, of ancestral passions. But this is perhaps looking rather far for an explanation. All Germans did not suddenly become barbarians again, but all go forward by choice or by force, to the automatic execution of a plan of campaign, reasoned, methodical, conceived in the Higher Command, and concerning which their military writers have always spoken very freely ; a war of extermination, of ravaging and massacres, in which terror plays its part, and fear empties entire regions at the approach of the armies. And, taking pleasure in the paradox, they say that to be cruel is in a way to be humane, because the suffering does not last so long, and, when all is reckoned, there are fewer victims.

It is undeniable that war inevitably brings excesses in its train ; no army can escape that fault. Where is the people which does not find sombre pages, under this head, in its history ? We have our own, which we do not forget.

But, with them, these crimes are not accidents, but a system. This savage conception of war is not the work of some excited men ; it arises in the mentality of military, political and intellectual circles ; it is the consequence of the Germanic Imperialism, that mad dream of universal domination which haunts every German brain ; it is

64

reasoned and thought out ; it presents itself under the cover, or it would be better to say under the banner, of a doctrine which engenders it and has the hardihood to justify it. From that they will not cleanse themselves.

They say they believe themselves to be the Superior Race, and they conclude therefrom that they have the right to supremacy, and that all means are good for them, even the worst, in order to impose it upon those who contest it. There is the principle.

All their military writers—Reimer, Bernhardi, Frymann, von der Goltz, Clausewitz, von Hartmann, and a score of others—extol these savage doctrines without shame.[1]

That there is no limitation upon violence and brutality in combat ; that moderation in war is an absurdity ; that the vanquished have no right to the preservation of their nationality and their language ; that war has for its end to kill and to destroy, and that consequently the more it kills and destroys the more closely it approaches its ideal ; that every atrocity which sows fear is legitimate from the simple fact that it contributes to the result by breaking the spirit of people ; that terrorism is a necessary feature of military procedure ; that war cannot be embarrassed with moral laws ; that the exigencies of humanity must bend before the necessities of war ; that war is the negation of the principles upon which civilization rests—all these are familiar aphorisms to be found in every page of their writings.[2]

A German officer, Walter Bloem, affirmed in the *Cologne*

---

[1] Cf. Reimer, *Pan-German Germany ;* Bernhardi, *Our Future,* and *Germany and the Next War ;* Frymann, *If I were the Kaiser ;* Clausewitz, *On War,* etc.

[2] Cf. Ch. Andler, " La Doctrine Allemande de la Guerre " (*Revue de Paris,* 15th January, 1915).

F

Gazette of the 10th February, 1915, that the atrocities of war form part of a system, and that a *Manual for the use of superior officers in enemy countries* indicates in detail the applications of this principle. And a well-known Member of the Centre Party, Herr Erzberger, has tranquilly declared that " war should be as pitiless as possible."

Clausewitz extols every means of injuring the enemy : first, invasion, not necessarily to conquer, but to devastate ; requisitions, of course, in order to be able to live, but also in order to exhaust and impoverish the country, and destroy it. " It is an error," he says, " to want to neglect the brutal element in war on the pretext that it is repugnant."[1]

We quote from William himself : " Humanity, for me, ends at the Vosges." And we are reminded that in 1900, haranguing his soldiers as they set out for China, he recommended them to leave nothing behind them, and to behave themselves as Huns.[2] Did he not write to the Austrian Emperor, at the beginning of the war, that stupefying letter which has been everywhere quoted : " My soul is harrowed, but it is absolutely necessary to put all to the fire and the sword, to kill men and women, children and old men, and not to leave standing a tree or a house. By these means of terror, the only means capable of striking a people as degenerate as the French, the war will be over within two months ; of that I am certain."[3]

There has been found, in an order of the day of the 26th August, 1914, prescribing the killing even of the wounded, without taking prisoners, this explanation by

[1] *Vom Kriege*, T. I, pp. 4, 15, 31.

[2] Cf. *Revue des Deux Mondes*, " Germany and the War," 15th October, 1914.

[3] *Bulletin de Legislation Comparée*, July, 1917, p. 421.

Pl. 33

Photo Doucet

THE REVERSE SIDE OF THE ENTRANCE (*see p.* 122; *face p.* 66)

Pl. 34

THE BURNED DOORS AND THE CALCINATED STONE-WORK OF THE INTERIOR
OF THE PORCH (ON THE PAVEMENT A PARTITION THROWN DOWN
BY A SHELL-EXPLOSION) (*see p. 122; face p. 67*)

General Stenger : " It is understood that we are not to leave a single enemy alive behind us."[1]

The King of Britain, in his message at the beginning of the war, was thus justified in saying, " The Germans have projected the destruction of the French nation."

And these atrocious doctrines have found their poets. Here is some poetry of Heinrich Vierordt which has been popular in Germany since the beginning of the war :—

" Now, Germany, hate !
With heart of iron, destroy in their millions the men of this devilish race.
Let their smoking flesh and shattered bones mount in piles to the sky, higher than the mountains !
Now, Germany, hate !
With resolve of steel, make no prisoners, and for each enemy a bayonet in the heart !
One after another, render them dumb.
Make a girdle of deserts of the countries around thee.
Now, Germany, hate ! "

" Instead of seeking to humanize war," writes M. Emil Boutroux, " they apply themselves to an infinite increase of its brutality . . . systematically and without putting any curb upon the brutal forces of cruelty and barbarity ; they reveal themselves the descendants of the Huns and Vandals, and let loose as widely as they can all the powers of evil."[2]

Finally comes the manifesto of the German " Intellectuals " to confirm this indictment with its avowal that nothing done by their army was an act of indiscipline : " *Keine zuchtlose grausankeit.*" It was done by order.

[1] *Revue de Paris*, 1st January, 1915, p. 65, Official Report. *Documents Relating o the War*, T. III, IV, No. 53, p. 66 ; No. 72, p. 72.

[2] " L'Allemagne et la Guerre," *Revue des Deux Mondes*, 15th October, 1914.

The war which they wage is a war of races, of people against people, which has less in view the conquering of the country as it is, the annexation of inhabited provinces, than the seizing of the soil of the naked earth, the adding of a new strip to the national territory, where they may instal themselves more at their ease, in the place of populations expelled or destroyed ; and " if the vanquished abandon their conquered lands, the ideal solution is reached, and everything possible should be done to bring it about."[1]

Germany's frontiers are confined ; she wants room. And Reimer, in his book *Pan-German Germany*, says that territorial conquest is not enough : the peoples who are in the way must disappear.[2]

They have not succeeded, after forty-four years of efforts and threats, in assimilating the Alsatians and Lorrainers, any more than they have the Poles of Silesia. They do not want that experience ever again. Hearts are harder to Germanize than stones.

As to Reims there is something more : the rude awakening from the German Dream brought about by Belgian heroism, the bitter ending to a boast, exasperated them into rage on the morrow of the " Miracle of the Marne."

It has seemed to me that these documented statements, showing the way in which the Germans conceive war, were

---

[1] Cf. Daniel Frymann, *If I were Emperor !*

[2] Cf. Reimer, *Pan-German Germany*. (Quoted in *La Revue*, October, 1914, p. 531.) Another author, Tanneberg, in his book *Greater Germany* (1911), recently translated into French under the title of *La Grande Allemagne*, forecasts a treaty to be imposed upon a vanquished France, under which within a year the inhabitants of the annexed departments, and even the French-speaking people in Belgium, shall abandon their native soil and go to France, so as to provide the Germans with territories free and empty. (Quoted in the *Temps* of the 12th March, 1914.)

Pl. 35

THE RAVAGED WINDOWS (ABOVE THE TRIFORIUM THE PRECIOUS GLASS
OF THE THIRTEENTH CENTURY) *(see p. 122; face p. 68)*

Pl. 36

THE HIGH THIRTEENTH-CENTURY WINDOWS (see p. 122; face p. 69)

worth insertion here, because they help us to understand, as well as their other crimes, the destruction of our Cathedral.

One thought all the same that face to face with Our Lady of Reims, at the moment of pointing their guns at that marvel of grace and power whose every chiselling is a prayer and each detail a work of art, the hands of the Prussian gunners would have trembled, that their commanders would have felt the human being rise up within them, that they would have hesitated, that they would not have dared. The grim soul of even a savage like Attila would have been moved.

When Von Molkte, from the heights overlooking Paris, saw, one fine morning in 1870 beneath the rays of the rising sun, the great city awaken, pensively he contemplated it, in its immensity, from the towers of Notre-Dame to the Arc de Triomphe, and he was heard to murmur, " One cannot destroy *that !* "

Molkte, on the hill of Bernu, facing the Cathedral of Reims, would have said the same : he would not have dared.[1]

Josias von Heeringen, in 1914, has dared !

After Louvain came the atrocious relapse at Reims ! And they knew what they were doing. For " this army, though heirs of old Germany, was not composed only of brutish boors and uneducated savages ; it comprised the entire people, with its *savants*, its artists, its book-compilers,

[1] Marshal von Molkte, in 1870, spent eight days at Reims, and old Rémois recall his frequent visits to the Cathedral. He never wearied of admiring it. They saw him more than once seated at the back of the choir, silent, his legs crossed, in contemplation before the Great Rose of the Front, forgetting, " in this spectacle of beauty, hard calculations and sanguinary visions."

its analysts, its minute annotators, whose patience and precision and method have made of Germany the country of erudition *par excellence*. They knew ; and yet they could do it ! "[1] The barbarians of other times had at least one excuse—ignorance. The Turks in 1453 did not destroy St. Sophia. And, if the Parthenon has been since 1687 no more than a ruin, that again was the work of a German soldier, in the pay of Venice, Wilhelm Otto von Koenigsmarck, who bombarded it.

Let us repeat it ; they have disavowed nothing. " Neither our troops nor we," wrote General von Ditfurth in the *Tag*, of Berlin, " owe explanations to any one ; we have nothing to justify, nothing to excuse. All that our soldiers will do to injure the enemy will be done properly, and has been justified in advance. We are not going to worry ourselves about the opinion of other countries, even neutral countries. *And if every monument, every masterpiece of architecture*, which is placed between our cannon and those of the enemy, *were sent to the devil*, that would be all the same to us. The most modest mound which is raised above the body of one of our warriors is more venerable than all the cathedrals and works of art in the world.[2] They regard us as barbarians ; what does it matter ? Let us laugh at them. Let them spare us once for all this idle chatter ; let them cease to talk of the Cathedral of Reims, or of churches or monuments which will share its fate. We do not wish to hear anything more. Only from Reims

[1] Ed. Harancourt, *Le Sacrilège*.

[2] On the morrow of the destruction of the *Lusitania*, which claimed 1145 victims, a Berlin journal, the *Post*, wrote : " Our adversaries will at length understand that the life of a single German soldier is dearer in our eyes than the *Lusitania* with all its passengers, with the Cathedral of Reims thrown in."

let there come to us the news of a second and victorious entry of our troops. The rest doesn't matter."[1]

Another, who has not this savage temperament of a beast of prey, but who has given proof of a singular lack of feeling, wrote to General Humbel :—

" I was far from thinking, as also were my compatriots, that the destruction of the Cathedral of Reims would be, on the part of the French, the subject of such unanimous reprobation. As a Lutheran, in reality a Free-thinker, I rejoiced in my hatred of Catholicism over the ruin of the churches of France, following on the Separation Law and the religious persecution. In delivering the blows of our cannon upon the Cathedral of Reims what have we done but work upon the same lines ? And now the French accuse us of vandalism ! . . .

" I know of course that this monument, apart from its religious character, has a historical and artistic value, but it appears to me that those are secondary considerations."[2]

Yet another, who does not care to seek for excuses, has declared : " When one has the force to create one has the right to destroy. We will rebuild it—their Cathedral—more beautiful, according to new designs, German designs."[3]

[1] Cf. the *Tag* of Berlin, quoted in the *Echo de Paris*, 28th October, 1914. To this savage literature, in so far as it concerns Reims Cathedral, we may add the following apostrophe by Von Klück, uttered in an access of anger to the inhabitants of a little town some days before the battle of the Marne : " We hold you. Your France is vanquished. Your Paris will be destroyed. We will not leave one stone upon another. Your monuments, your Arc de Triomphe, your Notre-Dame, your Louvre—we will destroy them all ; we will burn them all ! There will be naked earth. The crows will nest there. We hate your Paris ; we hate France. And we, the barbarians, will shew you that we *are* barbarians. (Quoted by M. Hanoteaux at the Sorbonne, 6th February, 1916, and published in the *Temps* of the 8th February.)

[2] Cf. *Libre Parole*, 26th September, 1914.

[3] Friedrich Gundolf, " Tat und Wort in Krieg," *Frankfurter Zeitung*, 11th October, 1914.

71

One must not give to this impudence greater weight than it deserves ; its very extravagance forbids us from regarding it as an expression of average German opinion.[1]

They are worth noting all the same, if only as a matter of curiosity, like that poetry in which impudence is reinforced by irony, which was published in a Berlin journal of standing.[2]

> " The Bells sound no more
> Beneath the double-towered dome,
> Benediction is over ! . . .
> With our lead, oh Reims,
> We have shut your idolatrous house.
> *Du schlossen mit Blei wir*
> *Dein Goetzenhaus, Rheims !* "

A document which carries more weight, and undoubtedly reflects the German Soul, is the " Appeal to the Civilized Nations "—the manifesto of the Ninety-three, addressed by the most eminent personalities in Letters, the Sciences and Arts to the journals of the whole world. So are the

[1] One cannot bring oneself to believe that in Berlin, as the correspondent of the *Daily Mail* asserted, " the news of the destruction of Reims Cathedral was welcomed by the public with great enthusiasm." (See the *Temps* of the 25th of September, 1914.) Yet at Bapaume, when they learned of the catastrophe, there was great joy in a German ambulance installed in the Communal School. A French soldier, M. D. de Paris, seriously wounded and ill, whose evidence I have myself collected, was broken in upon brusquely by his attendant, who, with a radiant air, exclaimed " Reims Kathedrale, Kaput ! " And all the Germans present displayed an indecent satisfaction.

[2] Rudolf Hertzog. See Art Supplement of the *Lokal Anzeuger*, for January, 1915. The reply of Catholics beyond the Rhine to the " French Attacks," written by Professor Rosenberg, expresses astonishment that we should have found an echo of German opinion in this verse—" the work of a mad fanatic spurned by every convinced Christian " (p. 109). It seems, nevertheless, that, if this literary effort was calculated to wound the susceptibilities of its readers, this journal, which is of a rather moderate character, would have refrained from publishing it in a special New Year Number.

protest of the twenty-two Universities,[1] of the " Professors of Higher Schools," and by the " Protestant Christians of Germany to Protestant Christians abroad," in which the intellectual élite of the nation unites itself with the military party.

They boil with indignation against the calumnies of which Great Germany is the victim. But they affirm that " the German Army and the German people are one " ; that " their militarism is inseparable from their civilization " ; that " there is no opposition between the spirit of German science and what is called Prussian militarism " ; that " the spirit which reigns in the German Army is the same as that which reigns in the German people."

So they disavow nothing. They explain ; and their explanations are only poverty-stricken arguments. They come too late. They constantly vary. They contradict one another.

So, on the 20th of September, 1914, M. Delcassé, Minister of Foreign Affairs, protested to the Governments of neutral States in these terms : " Unable to invoke the appearance of military necessity, and for the sole pleasure of destroying, the German troops have subjected the Cathedral of Reims to a systematic and furious bombardment. It is the duty of the Government of the Republic to denounce, for universal indignation, this revolting act of vandalism, which, in delivering to the flames a sanctuary of our history, robs humanity of an incomparable portion of its artistic patrimony." It is in vain for the Germans

---

[1] This protest is signed by the rectors of the Universities of Tubingen, Berlin, Bonn, Breslau, Erlangen, Frankfort, Fribourg, Giessen, Gottingen, Greifswald, Halle, Heidelberg, Jéna, Kiel, Koenigsberg, Leipzig, Marburg, Munich, Munstein, Rostoc, Strasburg and Würzberg.

to talk ; their interested and embarrassed allegations are worthless in the light of the facts. Neither on Saturday the 19th of September, nor on the preceding days, was there anything to justify the bombardment and burning of the Cathedral. Machine-guns were never mounted there against their aircraft, nor, for even stronger reasons, were guns put there, as a fantastic *communiqué* of the Wolff Agency would have us believe. There was nothing in the neighbourhood, still less inside, in the way of either men or war material. It was not used as a military post of observation.

True, it seems that just after the reoccupation of the town by the French troops, they had thought of making an observation from the towers on the 14th and 15th of September ; but in fact, and precisely out of fear of compromising the building, the project was renounced ;[1] and

---

[1] In August, *when the Germans were still in Belgium*, several attempts to instal wireless telegraphy were made ; but the installation was immediately afterwards transferred elsewhere.

On the morrow of the accident of which the airship *Dupuy de Lome* was the victim, still in the month of August, the Parc d'Aerostation attempted to instal a projector on the north tower in order to avoid a second mistake. The apparatus being much too feeble, only worked—and that with great difficulty—for a night or two. It had to be given up. There was nothing else even at that time—neither rifles, nor machine-guns, nor arms of any kind whatever—on the towers. The watchmen had at their disposal only simple rockets to announce the return of our aeroplanes or to give the alarm. And so little importance was attached to this temporary expedient that no one troubled even to remove the traces of it.

Even the manner in which this stage which offended the Germans was built is proof that one never thought of making it an observation post. One masks an observation post as much as possible ; the man on watch hides himself in his shelter, like a hunter in ambush. Now here nothing was masked, neither the staging nor the men. The staging extended over the tower, and the men stood out from it in full view. That is to say, if it had been desired, in September, to utilize for observation purposes this scaffolding, constructed in August for quite another purpose, it would certainly have been necessary to modify its arrangement.

The wire which was fixed there, and of which one could for a long time see the débris, was not telephone wire, but the wires of the projector for the light. The

it is literally true that from Tuesday the 15th of September in the evening, there was nothing, absolutely nothing, which could furnish the shadow of a pretext for the fire of the German batteries.

Now the Cathedral was not seriously bombarded until the 18th of September, for one cannot say that the three shells it received on Thursday the 17th constituted an intentional and systematic bombardment. Nevertheless, they cling desperately to the lie about " a post of observation." Not that embryo of the 14th and 15th, of which they do not even speak ; still less those abortive attempts in August, to which they make no allusion—but a post in active operation, threatening them, giving them trouble *hic et nunc*, on the 18th and the 19th, at the very moment when they fire upon it, because, in spite of themselves, they are forced to defend themselves against it.

On the 20th September the Official Press Agency of Berlin announces the events of the previous day in these terms :—

" We fired several isolated shots upon the Cathedral, to make the French understand that we would reduce it to cinders *if they persisted in bombarding us from that position.*

official report on the bombardment of the Cathedral, published in 1915, by the Minister of War in Berlin, errs when it contends that the Abbé Thinot had admitted in *l'Illustration* (of the 10th October, 1914) that there was a projector in activity on the tower on the night of the 13th September. M. Thinot said nothing of the kind. He alluded without any possibility of misapprehension to the above-mentioned attempt in August, " which was not persisted in, and in any case," he said, " was long before coming into contact with the enemy." The German Reporter interposed in the text of M. Thinot this date of the 13th September, which is not to be found there. Professor Rosenberg, in his " Reply," without observing any more scruple, has done the same thing.

During their own occupation in September, when they were fighting before Reims, the Germans did not hesitate to put a post of observation on the Cathedral.

As the enemy continued, the heavy artillery was ordered to destroy the Cathedral. After some shots the edifice caught fire."

On the 21st the German General Headquarters declared that there was a post of observation on the towers, fraudulently concealed *by the white flag*.[1] " We have been obliged to suppress this post by means of shrapnel fired by the field artillery. *The heavy artillery was not in action*, and the fire of our guns was stopped when the post had been destroyed."[2]

And indeed the north tower was badly knocked about on the 19th. Their shells were aimed accurately ; but behind those blocks of stone there was nothing and nobody —the Red Cross flag was their target. As to the " white flag," that had been removed since the morning of Sunday, the 13th.[3]

And if the heavy artillery which " *was ordered to destroy the Cathedral* " did not fire, whence came these enormous naval gun shells, those big high-explosive shells—the " 210's," the splinters of which we actually picked up on the spot ?

On the 22nd the Wolff Agency throws all the blame upon the French, " who had posted their guns on the approaches of the Cathedral and begun the fire."

On the 26th, moved—annoyed rather—by the cry of stupor and anger which burst forth like a curse against Germany from all quarters of the globe, the Imperial

---

[1] The *North German Gazette* of the 28th of September, takes the same line : " It is proved officially—and the French have not attempted to deny it—that the Cathedral of Reims has been used, under the shelter of the white flag, as an observation post."

[2] Berlin (official). See *Le Temps* of the 26th September, 1914.

[3] It was taken down by M. l'Abbé Dage and M. Guedét.

Pl. 37

Photo Thinot

THE GREAT ROSE AND THE GALLERY OF THE TRIFORIUM BENEATH
(see p. 122; face p. 76)

Pl. 38

Photo J. Matot

THE GREAT LUSTRE OF THE CHAPEL OF THE BLESSED SACRAMENT WHICH FELL THREE DAYS AFTER THE FIRE

(see p. 124; face p. 77.)

Chancellor tried to attenuate the impression by a note from his ambassador to the Spanish Government which stated that :—

" By reason of the careful observation which was being taken from the top of the Cathedral our infantry suffered such losses that the bombardment became inevitable. As the bombardment of this observation post by light artillery did not produce the desired effect, the German Staff found itself obliged, to its great regret, to fire *one shell from a mortar*, after which firing was stopped."[1]

The German *communiqué* of the 14th of October is aggressive. It prepares opinion (by the usual lie) for the succeeding bombardments in the second half of October.

" The French have installed *two batteries of heavy artillery* close to the Cathedral of Reims. It has been ascertained in addition that *light signals* have been made on one of the towers of this edifice. Of course our troops must adopt the measures necessary for assuring their defence without preoccupying themselves about the Cathedral. . . . *The French therefore will be responsible, now as before, for the renewed bombardment of the Cathedral.*"

Thus the lie is kept up.

The Rémois can say that they only know what passes on the top of the towers, particularly at night ; but it is a matter of public notoriety, and the entire population is a witness to it, that no battery of artillery of any kind was ever posted in the neighbourhood of the Cathedral.

On the 30th of October the Prussian Minister at Rome received the order to go and lie to the Pope.

" The French Staff having *again* placed a battery in

---

[1] War *communiqué*. Note to the Spanish Embassy. (Information from the *Handelstages*.)

front of Reims Cathedral,[1] and established on one of the two towers a post of observation, the Prussian Minister to the Holy See *has been charged by Herr Bethmann-Hollweg* to present a formal protest to the Holy See against such a method of abusing buildings consecrated to religious worship."[2]

Falsehood was finding its way into the Vatican, officially.

The Cardinal Archbishop of Reims considered a reply was necessary, all the more since the Imperial Chancellor had given to his diplomatic Note a comminatory conclusion : " Any damage *which may in the future be done to Reims Cathedral*, will fall upon the French, for it will be miserable hypocrisy to attribute it to the Germans."

His Eminence addressed to the Holy Father a Memorandum, with documents in support, and charged me to publish in the Press, by the same medium of the Havas Agency, a denial of this unspeakable German *communiqué*. It appeared in the papers on the 6th of November, 1914, as follows :—

" The entire press reproduced from a Havas telegram of the 31st October at least this passage—' The French General Staff having again placed a battery in front of the Cathedral, etc.'

[1] In order to lie usefully, one should maintain an appearance of truth. The Entrance of the Cathedral faces west. As the German positions extended from Brimont to Nogent-l'Abesse, i.e. from north to south by east, it would be physically impossible for a battery posted on the narrow Parvis to hit them.

A *communiqué* from the Great Headquarters of the Germans, dated the 21st of April, 1915, renewed this lie. " We recognized at a short distance from the Cathedral (*unweit der Kathedrale von Reims*) an enemy battery, and we subjected it to our fire."

[2] *Agence Havas*, 31st October. It is not inopportune to recall in this place that during the battle which was fought before Reims on the 11th and 12th of September, the Germans, who were in occupation of the town, did not scruple to " abuse buildings consecrated to religious worship," and that they placed an observation post on the North Tower of the Cathedral.

Pl. 39

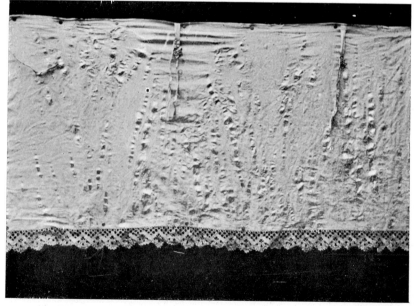

Photo M. Abelé

THE COMMUNION CLOTH SPOTTED WITH DROPS OF LEAD WHICH FELL THROUGH
THE FISSURES IN THE ROOF (see p. 124; face p. 78)

Pl. 40

Photo Thinot

THE SANCTUARY PAVEMENT

Photo Thinot

THE BURNED CHOIR-STALLS (*see p. 124; face p. 79*)

" The author of this note has been misled by his informants, and the error is too serious in its consequences to be allowed to pass unchallenged, particularly since the Cathedral, already devastated, is to be made to suffer again because of it.

" As witness hour by hour of what passes in my church, I am in a position to set out the facts with intimate knowledge of them, and it is my duty to do so.

" The note affirms that *again*—that is to say since the fire of the 19th of September—a battery has been placed in front of the Cathedral, and an observation post installed on one of the towers. In the name of His Eminence the Cardinal Archbishop of Reims and in my own name I testify that no battery has been placed on the Parvis, and that no observation post has been installed on the towers ; also that never at any moment have troops been encamped or stationed in any way in the proximity of the Cathedral.

" MAURICE LANDRIEUX,
" Vic.-Gen. and Archpriest of Notre-Dame."

The Wolff Agency maintained the lie doggedly ; and by order it stated : " The Wolff Agency *is charged to declare officially* that, contrary to the denials of M. Landrieux, the Archpriest, speaking in his own name and in that of the Cardinal, the presence of artillery near the Cathedral and of an observation post on the towers has been established on various occasions, and that the facts remain, despite all denials."[1]

[1] Berlin official. Cf. *Tribune de Genève,* 17th November, 1914. This same note was reproduced by a part of the Italian Press, which adopted it. (*La Stampa* of the 18th November.)

As for the *Neueste Nachricten* of Munich, it went still further : it was more—experienced. It informed its readers on the 10th of November that " according to a despatch from Berlin M. Landrieux, Vicar-General of Reims, has admitted that an observation post has been placed by the military authorities on the towers of the Cathedral, and that the Imperial Chancellor has immediately advised the Pope of these admissions."[1]

These threats of a fresh bombardment were not vain. The Cathedral received, in the following weeks, seventeen shells which were counted, some of which made considerable ravages, such as the shell which loosened the high gallery from the chevet over a length of eight metres, with a breach of four metres (Plate 61).

And that continues. *Communiqués* alternate with shells.

It would seem, so much breath do they expend over this observation post, as if the root of the matter were there, and that, if the French Army had not made it a citadel, the idea of destroying Reims Cathedral would never have occurred to them. It is we who forced them to it.

Then why did they bombard and destroy the Cathedral of Soissons ? Certainly there was at Soissons nothing of the kind which they allege at Reims,[2] and they did not attempt to get anything of the sort believed—until long afterwards. At the time they sought neither excuse nor pretext.

And on the 12th of October—was that also to suppress

[1] Quoted by *l'Echo de Paris*, 15th November, 1914.

[2] Concerning this I received the most formal assurance in writing from Mgr. Péchenard, the Bishop of Soissons, on the 4th March, 1915, and from M. Laudais, Archpriest of the Cathedral, on the 2nd October, 1916.

Pl. 41

Photo Thinot

FROM THE PORCH OF THE NORTH TOWER (THE STATUE OF OUR LORD)
(*see p.* 125; *face p.* 80)

Pl. 42

Photo J. Matot

ON THE ROOF: THE DISASTER (THE EXTRADOS OF THE ARCHING)

(see p. 126; face p. 81)

Pl. 43

Photo Doucet

Photo Doucet

THE GREAT ROOF : BEFORE AND AFTER (see p. 126; face p. 80 (a))

Pl. 44

GENERAL ASPECT OF THE ROOF (see p. 126; face p. 81 (a))

Pl. 45

THE GABLE OF THE GREAT ENTRANCE

Photo Thinot

THE GABLE OF THE SOUTH TRANSEPT
(WITH THE *SAGITTAIRE*)

THE GABLE OF THE NORTH TRANSEPT
(*see p. 126; face p. 80 (b)*)

Pl. 46

Photo Thinot

THE GREAT ARCHES AT THE CROSSING OF THE TRANSEPT (*see p.* 126; *face p.* 81 (b))

Pl. 47

Photo Thinot

DÉBRIS OF THE CARILLON (*see p. 127; face p. 80 (c)*)

Pl. 48

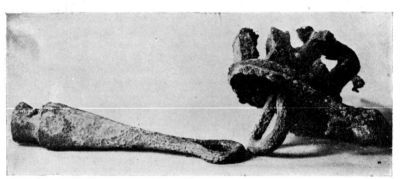

Photo Thinot

DÉBRIS OF THE SIXTEENTH-CENTURY BELL.
"THE BELL OF THE BLESSED SACRAMENT" (*see p.* 127; *face p.* 81 (c))

an observation post that they tried to injure Notre-Dame of Paris ?

Towards the end of November the journals beyond the Rhine published an explanatory note, with a plan, to establish definitely that it is we others—the French—who are responsible : first, because the unfortunate position of two batteries put the Cathedral in the line of fire of the fort of Nogent, and that it was not the fault of the gunners " if some of their shells went wide. It would have been worse if their shells had not been marvellously precise " ; secondly, because " the aeroplanes discovered not only the observation post, but, more important, an ammunition park on the Parvis." They have not yet seen this ammunition park, which is as much of a phantom as the big guns before the Entrance !

To us, then, they say that it is our fault. Amongst themselves, they have tried to make believe that it was our work ! The *Gazette de Lausanne* of the 30th September, 1914, reports that one of its correspondents passing through Berlin on the 23rd of September, " saw placarded on the walls immense posters representing the ruins of the Cathedral, with this inscription : ' This is how the French destroy their monuments.' " One is disarmed in presence of this German tenacity in lying ![1]

The *Internationale Monatschrift* of December, 1914, brings us a pearl which we must gather even at the risk of unduly elongating this fantastic display of duplicity and audacity.

[1] On the 12th July, 1916, nearly two years after the event, a German journal serenely wrote : " The French place the degradation of Reims Cathedral to the account of German barbarity."—*Deutsche Tages Zeitung.*

G

The Cathedral of Reims

In a sensational article on " the protection of monuments of art in war-time " with which neutral countries were inundated, we are made acquainted with the solicitude of the Kaiser and his Government for our churches and cathedrals, which must be protected, in respect to our marvellous treasures of art and our old churches, against the inconceivable negligence of our Government, as witness M. Maurice Barrès' book, *La Grande Pitié des Eglises de France*.[1]

The author, Counsellor P. Clémen, President of the Section of Historic Monuments of the Rhenish Provinces and commissary of the Civil Administration, was commissioned to inspect the artistic monuments of the invaded territories in Belgium and France. Reims Cathedral is not in the zone of occupation, but he had a mission never-

---

[1] The Conservator of the Royal Library of Bavaria, Dr. Pfeiffer, plunges still more heavily into impudence : " This admirable monument of Reims," he says, " has been neglected, and damaged, in an incredible manner by the absolute carelessness and unintelligence of the French authorities and the State. . . . Those who have seen Reims Cathedral know this : holes in the walls were hidden under Gobelins ; and with regard to the statues on the exterior, Voeges wrote, not long since, words which should make our accusers blush : ' How disgraceful it is thus to leave these precious witnesses of the history and art of France to perish by wet and wind.' One need not be a prophet to foresee that the reparation of the damage caused by the bombardment will be the occasion of a complete renovation of the Cathedral which will permit it to appear in its pristine splendour, and will efface the traces of the carelessness of its French guardians." (Cf. *La Suisse*, 1st November, 1914.)

He also pretends to justify the bombardment on the plea of the installation of guns near the Cahedral, and of the observation post, in September and October, and he adds that the Place du Parvis, " was continually used as a camp for the troops and as a munition dump." (See *The Bombardment of Reims Cathedral*, by Dr. Maximilien Pfeffer.)

Another, Dr. Karl Frey, Counsellor of State and Professor at the University of Berlin, declares, in the *Gazette of the Cross*, that " even the complete destruction of Reims Cathedral would have no great importance, because cathedrals can be rebuilt. And as we know their structure down to the smallest details, we are sure of a successful reconstitution." (Quoted in the *Grande Revue*, March, 1915, p. 77.)

Pl. 49

DÉBRIS OF THE ANGELUS BELFRY *(see p. 127)*

Photo Thinot

THE SPIRE OF THE ANGELUS BELFRY WHICH FELL ON THE LOWER ROOF
(see p. 127; face p. 82)

Pl. 50

Photo Thinot

CALCINATED STONES AT THE FIRST STAGE OF THE NORTH TOWER

(see p. 128; face p. 83)

theless to pronounce a judgment and give his opinion upon it, and he confided to the *Lokal Anzeiger* of Berlin the conclusions arrived at in his report, and which are before me as I write.

After informing us that they have heard in Germany enough " of the shrieks of Frenchmen and the jeremiads of neutrals, about that Cathedral," he also does not hesitate to declare that everything that happened is our doing,[1] but that in the result what did happen was no great matter. " I was able," he says, " with disconcerting completeness to examine the monument on a clear December morning, by the aid of the telemeter at a distance of 5 kils. 500."[2]

But what about the rigorous precision of German scientific methods now ? An expert examination at five kilometres distance ![3]

[1] The army of Von Heeringen was forced to defend itself, since heavy batteries had been installed in front of the Cathedral, with a white flag on the towers. " The fact," he says, " has been established without contest.

" On our battle front there was, perhaps, in the trenches a young Goethe, a young Beethoven. Frankly, would not the world and civilization have suffered more from the death of this young Goethe than from the destruction of a cathedral ? "

Dr. Clemen is comparatively moderate. The deputy Erzberger goes farther when he declares " that to annihilate London would be more humane than to let a single German lose his blood on the battlefield." (Quoted by M. Prüm in his Letter to German Catholics.)

Nevertheless they are not barbarians. " It is the German spirit which makes the war, and not German militarism. Our intellectuals, our scientists, our poets, our architects and our sculptors, our historians and our art critics are also in the Army. Before Reims German troops are commanded by a general who has made a name for himself by his studies in the history of art." (P. Clemen, *Internationale Monatschrift*.)

[2] About three and a half miles. *Lokal Anzeiger*, 7th January, 1915.

[3] M. C. Eulart, director of the Museum of Comparative Sculpture of the Trocadéro, and member of the Commission on Historical Monuments, has rated this report at its proper worth. " Monument of falsehood and impudence, the odious and grotesque imbecility of which only a German mind could fail to comprehend ! A man up to now esteemed for his good work, Dr. Paul Clémen, has been made ridiculous by the German Emperor with the title of Inspector of Monuments of the Occupied

It may be noted that though, from the German positions to the north and north-east of Reims, one can see the chevet of the Cathedral, the transept and a part of the aisles, it is physically impossible from any spot whatever between Brimont and Nogent to get even an oblique view of the part of the building which faces west.

He therefore saw the Cathedral from behind, and dares to talk of the Entrance !

He knows and proclaims that the Cathedral was only touched by two projectiles, one of fifteen, and the other of twenty-one centimetres."[1]

Now at that date there was lying on the arches an un-exploded shell—a 150 : so it would be that which alone had caused all the damage !

He is also very categorical on the subject of the observation post. They will not give that up.

But one has reason to be astonished all the same that after the formal declarations of the Cardinal Archbishop of Reims, the Chapter of Cologne should make this in-destructible lie its own. In a note in the *Cologne Gazette*, communicated to the Press of neutral countries, after declaring, as it had a right to do, that Cologne Cathedral had never been used as an observation post, it adds, " The dome of Cologne, unlike that of Reims, has nothing to do with military operations. It serves only the divine service.

Countries, and he has degraded himself so far as to permit himself to sign a complaisant report upon Reims Cathedral, which he admits having only seen through glasses at a distance of five kilometres. That was sufficient for him to affirm officially that the Entrances have not suffered." (Cf. *La Cathedrale de Reims. L'Art et les Artistes,* special number, p. 10.)

[1] In December at the time of this famous examination, the Cathedral had received not two, but at least sixty-three shells.

Pl. 51

Photo Thinot

THE TOP OF THE NORTH TOWER

(AT THE END OF NOVEMBER, 1914)   (AT THE END OF JANUARY, 1915) (see p. 128; face p. 84)

Pl. 52

Photo J. Matot

CURIOUS EFFECT OF THE BLAST OF A SHELL AT THE SUMMIT OF ONE OF THE
SPIRES OF THE NORTH TOWER *(see p. 128)*

Photo Doucet

THE SPIRE WITH ITS COVER (ON THE LEFT—SEE ILLUSTRATION ABOVE)
(face p. 85)

Perhaps it is simply desired, by these groundless accusations, to excuse the effective utilization of Reims Cathedral for military purposes."[1] Clearly we have to deal with an obsession.[2] It is true that if they abandoned it, they would have nothing left to say : they would no longer in the face of Notre-Dame figure as soldiers, but would show themselves as bandits. However, they cannot deceive anyone.

In respect to the 17th, the 18th and the 19th of September, they have witnesses whom they cannot reject—their own wounded, who encumbered the approaches of the tower—even of both towers—and obstructed the staircase. They would declare, I am sure, because it was evident to

---

[1] Cf. *Koelnische Volkszeitung*, quoted by the Swiss journal *Der Bünd*, 22nd February, 1915.

It may be that this assertion has no more foundation in respect to Cologne than it has in respect to Reims, but it is, to say the least, unfortunate that the *Nieuwe Courant* of Rotterdam could reply to this lofty pleading *per Domo*, by exhuming a forgotten article in the *Rhenische Westphalische Zeitung* of the 4th August, 1914 (No. 923), where, dealing with the military measures taken for the defence of Cologne, it is said that " machine-guns have been placed on the turrets of bridges, as well as on the *towers of the Cathedral* " ; also that a great English journal should have been enabled to receive and publish this very categorical statement from one of its correspondents : " Machine-guns are in position on the roofs of several houses, and also on the towers of the Cathedral. In spite of official denials I am certain of this ; one of my compatriots, who lives in Cologne, has seen them fire, on two occasions, upon enemy aeroplanes."

In a well-documented account of a visit to Strasbourg in 1916 the American journalist, Mr. Thomas Curtin, made similar statements : " The glorious old sandstone Cathedral, with its gorgeous façade, and lace-like spire, had a Red Cross flag waving over the nave ; and a wireless apparatus was installed on the spire. Sentries passed backwards and forwards on the uncompleted tower which dominates the region to the Vosges." (*Times*, 22nd November, 1916.)

In February, 1919, General Hirschauer, military governor of Strasbourg, in a report to Marshal Pétain, confirmed this information officially.

[2] In June, 1917, a German " Albatross " was brought down by one of our machines in the Montagne de Reims. The lieutenant-observer, Kurt Tzollhorn, who was wounded, affirmed to M. B., a priest stretcher-bearer of the 38th Corps, who reproached him for the blind fury of their bombardment of the Cathedral, that he knew the reason for it, that he had " *seen with his own eyes* when flying over Reims,

them, that not one soldier attempted to mount there, and that, besides, there were neither French officers nor French soldiers in the Cathedral during those days, except some men who were posted on guard, and remained, outside.

And everyone knows that never, not for a single day, since the fire has the Cathedral been reopened to the public (Plate 60); that the Rémois have not set foot in it; that it has been shut since that time; that strangers can only enter for a few moments, and are always accompanied; that access to the towers is rigorously forbidden by the

not only the post on the towers, but the batteries surrounding the Cathedral!" And nothing would induce him to give up his belief.

But he was a German. In May, 1918, the Wolff Agency brought forward evidence which should appear less suspect, and " could not be challenged," it said : A French officer, Edouard Albert de Bondelli, declared that in 1917 he had directed the observation post on the Cathedral. Now, after enquiry, the *Journal de Génève* discovered traces of this officer, Edouard Albert de Bondelli, but he had died in 1910, at the age of forty-nine years, leaving two sons, of whom one, in the Army, had not been to the front in April, 1917, while the other was under military age.

The enquiry by Colonel Feyler, the report of which this same journal has given, has more importance. The German *communiqué* of the 11th March affirmed that a *poste d'optique* had on several occasions been worked on the Cathedral. The next day two Deputies, Messrs. Abel Ferry and Renaudel, went to Reims to examine the matter *de visu :* they established the inanity of the accusation. The Cardinal, in concert with the military authorities, had again issued a formal denial, explaining, quite candidly, that the architect had been obliged to execute certain works of preservation half-way up the north transept, sufficiently visible to give no excuse for the Germans to misunderstand them. A German radiogram of the 19th of March had replied " that the Cardinal does not spend the night on the towers, and that it was easy to suppress the post during his visit, and re-establish it afterwards."

It was then that Colonel Feyler, who happened to be in France, wished to clear the matter up. Arriving unexpectedly in Reims, on the 20th, without telling anyone of his coming, he asked on the spot permission to make an immediate inspection. The civil guard who accompanied him was ordered to take him everywhere. And he declared that he could not discover, in spite of his investigations in the capacity of an expert military inquisitor, " *anything which from far or near resembled an observation post, or the slightest trace of what could be one, not even any débris of maps or records or anything which could indicate that any installation of that kind had ever existed.*" He added that " *the aspect of neglect and the forsaken appearance of the north tower* had struck him particularly."

military authorities, no matter to whom, and even, and above all, to officers ; that the doors of the stairs are closed ; and that, rather than authorize some workmen to go on the roof where some urgent work of preservation was needed, the State resigned itself to seeing the disaster aggravated by rain, wind, and frost, the ceilings remaining bare through four winters—they are so still[1]—precisely in order not to furnish to the bad faith of the Germans the shadow of a pretext, and to oblige them to lie again, and to lie without cessation, in saying that which they persist in saying.

There is an official document, the famous Report of the Minister of War,[2] published at Berlin in 1915, which because of its origin and character must not be passed over. It swarms with errors.

It makes its own all the stories : the artillery park (p. 6) ; the heavy batteries in the town (p. 15), behind and to the right of the Cathedral (p. 8), on the neighbouring Place (p. 7), and its immediate vicinity (pp. 6, 9 and 16) ; the assembling of infantry on the Parvis (p. 14) ; the projector on the towers on the 13th September (p. 5), and again after the fire (p. 19) ; signals with flags on the 19th (pp. 14, 15, and 18) ;[3] finally and always—a military

[1] In his official Report on the ravaged monuments of Belgium, Dr. Paul Clemen complaisantly remarks that in regard to the buildings burned or bombarded at Malines, Louvain and other places care has been taken that all work of protection— temporary cover, the stopping of holes, the mending of broken windows, the riveting of walls—should be done before the winter.

Reims Cathedral did not benefit by this solicitude.

[2] *Kriegsministerium. Die Beschiessung der Kathedrale von Reims*, Berlin, 1915.

[3] Neither on Saturday the 19th nor on the previous evening, was there any movement of flags on the tower. On Thursday morning we had been obliged to hoist the Red Cross flags, an operation which necessarily implies movements, which they could see. But those movements were not signals, and they did not look like signals. A child could not misunderstand them. Besides, on that day, the 17th, they do not speak of it.

87

post of observation on the 18th and 19th on the north tower (pp. 6, 7, 12, 14, and 18).

These falsehoods are not cumulative ; they get in each other's way, and neutralize one another ; there are too many of them. It is not, however, this rehash of 1914 *communiqués* that it is my purpose to reproduce here, but certain statements and certain reflections, reading which makes one rub one's astonished eyes. I will call attention to three only :—

I. They declare that *it was expressly forbidden to bombard the Cathedral* (p. 8) ; *that on the 19th of September, a single shot from a mortar was fired at the Cathedral at 12.20* (pp. 7, 14, and 18) ;[1] that *that was the only time it was directly aimed at* (p. 8) ; that *on the 22nd or the 23rd, batteries having been observed by aircraft quite close to the Cathedral, a shot was fired without being aimed at the building*, and that consequently *if it was struck it was unintentionally, because the objective was in the immediate vicinity* (pp. 8 and 16) ; that *they never afterwards fired on the Cathedral, but only on the enemy positions* (p. 8).[2]

The answer to these audacious statements has been

[1] The Cathedral, which had already been struck thirteen times the day before and thrice the day before that, received on Saturday the 19th at least twenty-four shells.

[2] They said just the same about Soissons Cathedral—mistake, error in taking the range. But there was found in the note-book of the Commander of a battery the *Ringkanonenbatterie*, to the north of Soissons, the following significant entries :—

31st January, 1915.—" The battery has fired 19 time-fuse and percussion shells on Soissons Cathedral. The spire and nave were hit several times."

2nd February, 1915.—" From 9.30 to 10.30 the Stenger battery fired on the Cathedral, and in particular on the spire, 29 shrapnel shells, 16 of which were hits."

25th February, 1915.—" Shells in stock, 199 ; consumption, 21 (Cathedral)."
Havas. (See *La Croix*, 15th April, 1917.)

88

written by their guns ; it is scored and engraved by the steel of shells in the stone of the building ; and in photographing those wounds one by one, we have counted the blows. Their denials will not prevail against these documents.

II. " The fire," they say again, " *was caused by the burning scaffolds of neighbouring houses* (pp. 8, 9, and 14). . . . *The entire responsibility for the damage falls upon the French. . . . It was not the bombardment but the scaffolds which set fire to the Cathedral. For some hours they let them burn, without doing anything to extinguish the fire ! . . . They even had the inconceivable negligence not to put the marvellous Treasure of the Cathedral in a place of safety* " (p. 9).

So this is what they have discovered after a year of reflection ! The burning of the Cathedral was only an accident ! They have nothing to do with it ! The fire spread—one does not know how—from the neighbouring houses.[1] Is it their fault, if these Rémois did not put it out ? these negligent Rémois, who would not even take the trouble to put their wonderful Treasure in a place of safety !

It is the incendiary who accuses the firemen. A pitiful

---

[1] Except the fire-brigade station, in the Rue Trudaine, which is on the other side of the Place du Parvis, there was no house burning at this time in the neighbourhood of the Cathedral. The Archbishop's Palace, the Convent of the Adoration, and the Maison Prieur did not catch fire until later, after the Cathedral, and set on fire by it.

It was not the scaffolding which set fire to the woodwork. The witness Prullage indicates that the sparks from the fire-brigade post had set fire to the straw, and that the conflagration was propagated from the naves to the outside ; it is absolutely certain that the scaffolding was on fire before the straw.

argument, which denies the facts, and which history will not admit !

III. They have dared to write this : " *It was a diabolical plan of cowardice and baseness to put the German wounded in the Cathedral, in order to shelter an observation post under the Red Cross, hitherto piously respected by all nations* " (p. 10). The German soul reveals itself completely, shamelessly, in this stupefying phrase, of whose indecency they are perhaps unaware. For, apart from the facts, of which they cannot be ignorant, that this idea of assembling their wounded in the Cathedral came from themselves, that the straw was brought there for that purpose, on their formal orders by requisition, and that if they did not themselves instal their wounded there, it was because their flight on the 12th of September did not leave them time to do it, it is an insult to the public mind or an aberration of the moral sense to count themselves, after what they have done, in the ranks of the nations " who piously respect the flag of the Red Cross."

I declare once more that never at any moment did the Cathedral ambulance serve as cover for an observation post. This accusation is more than a lie ; it is an outrage.

This accumulation of falsehoods, these artful pleas, at length become wearisome ; yet it is necessary to follow them up to the end, and say a word more concerning another voluminous work, of nearly five hundred pages, written with more of passion than critical accumen— *German Culture, Catholicism and the War*,[1] which has been distributed profusely in neutral countries.

[1] A reply to the French work *La Guerre Allemande et le Catholicisme*. Published, in collaboration, by Georg Pfeilschifter, 30th November, 1915.

Chapter IX, under the title, " War, Art and the Sanctuaries," discusses the question of ravaged towns, and particularly Reims and Louvain. The author, a theologian, Dr. J. Sauer, deals with the whole matter of the Cathedral. The chapter is a new edition of the famous Ministerial Report. He reproduces all its false statements, he adopts all its conclusions, but he introduces certain comments and arguments, to the boldest only of which I wish to draw attention.

He loses himself at the start in a maze of endless considerations ; he accumulates texts to establish his point that religious edifices have no right of protection in time of war, according to the 27th article of the Hague Convention, except " on condition of not being used for military purposes " ; and he accuses us " of having coldly calculated on the German sentiment for Art " in sheltering in our churches, and, in the present case, in the Cathedral, observation posts and machine-guns. " Doubtless," he says, " they hoped that we should charge our guns with woollen balls and our rifles with cotton bullets " (p. 185).

These lengthy dissertations are to no purpose. Nobody disputes the principle. It is not the principle, but the facts, which we contest. And, whatever they may say, and in spite of their denials, they have bombarded and burned the Cathedral, though it was not " used for military purposes."

That is the whole point. There is no other question.

The history of the bombardment is written thus. " Already, during the general bombardment of the town on the 18th of September, a *misdirected* projectile from a 15 centimetre howitzer had struck the roofing of the Cathedral, and damaged some of the pediments " (p. 217).

" On the morning of the 19th, the immediate neighbourhood of the church, *where large concentrations of troops had been established*, was shelled by our artillery. The shrapnel fire upon the observation post in the north tower not having given sufficient results, at midday a mortar launched upon it a projectile which struck the tower on the right. *That is the only case where the Cathedral itself was made an objective* " (p. 218).

" In the afternoon the scaffolding caught fire, from the flames from neighbouring houses our High Command *supposes*—from the direct action of an incendiary shell the French narrative pretends. Admitting this last hypothesis, the projectile in question *was intended for another objective*, since it is stated that on that day not a single shell, other than that from the mortar, was directed against the Cathedral."

Finally, " after the first bombardment (that of the 19th) on the 22nd or 23rd of September (p. 218) a shell aimed at a battery established behind the Cathedral, struck *the burnt roof unintentionally without any fault of aim*. The Minister of War energetically contests any other direct or voluntary shelling of the Cathedral. If still other projectiles did hit the edifice, *it was the effect of pure chance* " (p. 220).

And that is all. Nothing further is said about the bombardment.

So the complete story, for those who read this big book of four hundred and ninety pages, published at the end of November, 1915, and intended to rectify history among the Neutrals, is that the Cathedral received, all told, four shells—on the 18th September, a stray shell ; on the 19th, the one and only official shell, which was deliberately

Pl. 53

Photo Thinot

THROUGH A SHELL-HOLE, IN THE SOUTH TOWER
(VIEW OVER THE PLACE ROYALE. GERMAN TRENCHES ON THE HORIZON)

(see p. 128; face p. 92)

Pl. 54

Photo Poirier

SPRING OF FLYING BUTTRESS, BROKEN AT THE ANGLE OF THE
NORTH TRANSEPT, AND THE APSE (18TH SEPTEMBER, 1914) (see p. 129)

Photo Thinot

SOME *DEBRIS* ON THE LOWER ROOFS OF THE APSE (see p. 129; face p. 93)

aimed for a special purpose ; a third, perhaps in the evening, very hypothetical, which in any case was meant for another objective ; and finally, on the 22nd or the 23rd, a fourth, which had lost its way. And if, afterwards, there were any others which took the same direction, " the Minister of War gives his word that it was the effect of pure chance."

Now, on Friday the 18th—after the three of the day before—it was not one shell, but thirteen, that struck the Cathedral ; the next day, *when the immediate neighbourhood was absolutely deserted, and there was not the smallest assembly of troops*, we noted twenty-five at least ; and on the 24th there were three. As to those which followed, by " an effect of pure chance," they amounted, at the end of November, 1915, to exactly forty-eight. And, be it remembered, they have repeatedly told us that " the fire of their batteries is marvellously precise." They must feel strongly the need of pleading extenuating circumstances when they descend to such miserable excuses.

Professor Sauer adopts the theory of fire from the neighbouring houses with a wise reserve however. Thus : " The scaffolding began to burn, set alight by the fire of the neighbouring houses, our High Command *supposes*."

But, if he brings no new element into the discussion of the facts, he at any rate establishes the responsibility with serene ingenuity and unrivalled assurance. I quote without comment. After having spoken of " irreparable damage " caused by the fire, he declares that *the fault must be attributed exclusively to the incredible negligence of the authorities responsible for the town of Reims*.

" It would have been easy, from the 12th to the 18th of September, to protect the entrances and the façade with sandbags. . . . Not a single measure was taken in view of fire, not even the most primitive. When the fire broke out, not an engine was put in action. The neighbouring fire-brigade station had been destroyed by a shell—intentionally, if we are to credit the French version. . . . As to the other fire stations, they did not apparently give themselves much trouble ; or can it be that in this town of 120,000 inhabitants there was only one station ? In any case such carelessness is absolutely inexcusable . . ." (p. 219).

They do not realize that their astonishment recoils upon themselves, and that the fault with which they reproach us is of not having taken them for what they are, of having believed that, if not the Faith, at any rate Art and History would suffice to protect Our Lady of Reims, and so of not seeing the need to guard against the blow.

Finally, we must record a recent note (5th June, 1918) from the Great German Headquarters to Cardinal Gasparri, setting out to the Holy See, *over the signature of Von Hindenburg*, some facts concerning the use of the Cathedral for war purposes, between June, 1917, and March, 1918.

Sometimes it is an observation post, sometimes there is signalling by lights ; at other times shadows which come and go ; *delle ombre che si muovevana sulla torre posta a sud ;*[1] but, most often, it is a wireless installation. This is new ; they have not formulated this accusation before.

They have seen, then, on the south tower[2]—up to that time it had been the north tower with which they

---

[1] I have only the Italian translation of the document.

[2] Since April, 1917, I have seen it with my own eyes, and Colonel Feyler noted it in the report of his enquiry on the 3rd April, 1918, that the upper staircase in each tower was demolished in such a fashion and to such an extent, that we can say that the summit is inaccessible.

Pl. 55

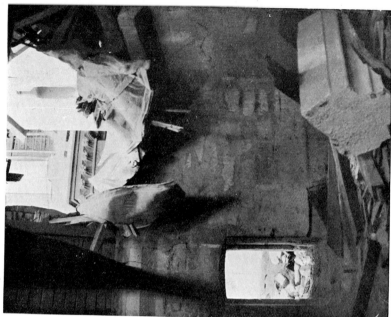

Photos Thinot

ROOF BROKEN IN BY THE FALL OF THE FLYING BUTTRESS—Pl. 54 (see p. 129; face p. 94)

Pl. 56

FLYING BUTTRESS STRUCK AT THE APSE, AND RIDDLED WINDOW

(18TH SEPTEMBER, 1914) *(see p. 129; face p. 95)*

concerned themselves—" some rods, *delle stanghe*, which resembled sail-yards, *che facevano sospettare un' antenna*," or rather, " a large apparatus which might be a wireless instrument, *forse attrezzi per radiotelegraphia*." In November they discovered " some sail-yards on the south tower, *la presenza, dell'antenna della torre* " ; then again in December, on the 7th, the 11th, and the 17th, they saw " the arm wire, *filo di ferro*,[1] which extended from one tower to the other, and two rods which had the look of sail-yards, *all' apparenza antenne* " ; on the 9th, the 13th, and the 18th, their observers intercepted wireless in the air, " *fu scoperta la radiographia*, which, in their estimation, *che a loro guidizio*, could only have come from the Cathedral, *non poteva che veniza da una torre della Cathedrale*." The witnesses " *son pronti a guirare la loro deposizione*." But how can they swear, except according to " *their estimation*," that it could only have come from the Cathedral ?

There are two big pages of this evidence, with dates and hours.

Really, if they had not lied so much, if one did not know that with them, in these matters, the morality of acts is referred, like everything else, to *Deutschland über alles*, that everything which is of service to Germany is good, and that that only is immoral which is of a nature to injure them, one would be troubled by such precision, and would at least give them credit for some good faith. But, whether there be good faith or not in the depths of their conscience, it is proved that on the towers of Notre-Dame there was

---

[1] The military wireless services use a wire of $1\frac{1}{2}$ mm., and it is unlikely that a field-glass could discover it at six or seven kilometres distance. Aerial photography cannot even get it at five hundred metres.

nothing ; that the facts did not correspond with their statements, and that everything which they affirm is objectively false.

On the 8th of September, 1918, the general commanding the Fifth Army, to whom the Cardinal had communicated a note of the German Great Headquarters of the 9th of July, when the charge was first formulated, and which was based on the hypothesis that some of the shooting of our batteries must have been directed from the Cathedral, replied :—

" Your Eminence knows as well as I do that not a single observation post, permanent or temporary, exists on Reims Cathedral.

" The employment of aeroplanes and balloons for directing and observing artillery fire makes the organization of an observatory on the Cathedral quite useless, as much so as from the Church of St. Rémi, which has suffered the same fate, and the proof invoked by the German note has in a military view no value whatever. It is merely a reason advanced for the purpose of trying to justify an unjustifiable act.   (Signed) " BERTHELOT."

On the morrow of the catastrophe their quibbles and " their falsehoods " might impress opinion, especially foreign opinion ; to-day they no longer find willing ears.

The value of their word and their own estimation of it has been revealed to us in those phrases of the Imperial Chancellor, uttered in the Reichstag on the 4th of August, 1914 : " *Necessity knows no law*," and " *One extricates oneself from an awkward position as best one can.*"

So long as they reckoned upon victory they scarce

troubled to excuse their misdeeds. " Glory will wash away everything," they said. Since the wind has changed, and the horizon has clouded, they see themselves under the *necessity* of escaping, at any cost, from their responsibility, and they extricate themselves from the business " as best they can." They contest, they deny, they explain, they accuse : anything is good enough which may put their accusers off the track. But they have lied too long, and " their falsehoods " are believed no more.

The hour will soon come, if it has not already sounded, when one will refuse any discussion with them ; they are for ever disqualified.

Pl. 57

Photo Sainsaulieu

TURRET OF THE 5TH COUNTERFORT (SOUTH SIDE), HALF BROKEN DOWN
(SHELL OF 18TH SEPTEMBER, 1914).   A COLUMN OF THE 4TH COUNTERFORT
BROKEN BY THE "210" WHICH ENTERED WITHOUT EXPLODING, AT
THE LION D'OR (8TH APRIL, 1915) (*see pp. 129 and 139; face p. 98*)

Pl. 58

A GARGOYLE SPITTING OUT LEAD, AT THE SOUTH-WEST ANGLE OF THE TRANSEPT

(see p. 130; face p. 99)

IV

THE OUTRAGE TO FRANCE AND TO OUR LADY

Pl. 59

Photo Thinot

THE BELLS MELTED OR BROKEN (*see p.* 131; *face p.* 100)

Pl. 60

Puget

THE RIGHT PORCH OF THE GREAT ENTRANCE—THE ONLY ENTRANCE TO THE
CATHEDRAL SINCE THE FIRE (*see p.* 86; *face p.* 101)

CHAPTER IV

THE OUTRAGE TO FRANCE AND TO OUR LADY

IF the fire at the Cathedral had been accidental, as in 1481 ; if it had been the mad work of a maniac or an idiot, or even of a bandit, the catastrophe would have been the same, and the same throb of poignant emotion would have thrilled the world. But there is no question here of accident. The incendiary is not a private individual, not one of those irresponsible degenerates whom one classifies as " abnormal." It is a people which has done this thing, in cold blood, a people which prides itself on being in the first rank among the peoples, and which is devoured with the ambition of being the people-type, the head among peoples—it is Germany !

When the first sensation of stupor had passed the world felt a convulsion of anger and disgust, which the Press registered, as the seismograph registers the quakings of the earth.

In face of such a crime, which in itself can find no justification, and which the calculations and necessities of military strategy do not suffice to explain, one gets, in spite of oneself, the impression that its meaning must be hidden in some higher idea ; one has the presentiment that, if one could read behind the act the secret thought of the German soul, its full meaning would be displayed, and one would discover the point where it touches a providential plan for

101

the execution of mysterious designs, which are really merciful designs. For, elsewhere in life, upon all the Calvaries where redemptions are wrought, human malice intrudes, and whilst it betakes itself to its task of hate, it nevertheless labours, though without merit and unwittingly, at a work of salvation. The more one reflects the less does one resign oneself to see, in those events of September, merely the blind and brutal effect of the chances of war.

It was not the stones which the Germans wanted to break down ; those stones did not annoy her ; it was Our Lady of Reims, with the great memories which she incarnates and represents ; our Cathedral, symbol expressing the greatness of France, and reliquary of our national glories.

The stake in this war is the nation's salvation—the independence, the honour, the life even, of France ; the revenge for 1870 ; the defence of Christian civilization against an aggressive return to barbarism ; it is peace, through the crushing of an insatiable race of prey, which makes itself an anarchist in trampling beneath its feet not only diplomatic treaties, but that international concordat which we call " the right of nations." It is yet one other thing : the lifting up of our country through expiation.

There are words which cost something to say, and to which some ears refuse to listen.

But must we not take to ourselves the grave lessons which Cardinal Mercier lately addressed to the Belgian people, with an apostolic freedom so fine and so noble that Christianity throughout the world raised its head to hear them. " It would be cruel," he said, " to dwell upon our own wrong-doing at the moment when we are expiating it so hardly and with such grandeur of soul ; but should we not avow that we have something to expiate ? "[1]

That God will save us we cannot doubt ; but that the salvation will reach us through the austere ways of repentance and redemption also appears evident.

When Justice strikes to chastise it strikes upon the back, it matters not where, just as it comes. When Mercy strikes to heal, it seeks the heart, for penitence is essentially suffering of the heart. And it is only when it sees this sorrowful breaking of the heart, in humility and under trial, that God pardons. *Cor contritum et humiliatum, Deus, non despicies.* But where does the heart of France beat ? Surely everywhere. From the Pyrenées to the Vosges, from the Alps to the ocean, in the city and in the fields, in Paris as in the provinces, one feels its pulsations ; it is the same blood which vivifies the whole organism. But if one takes historic realities as the test one turns to Reims, when one speaks of the heart of France.

Paris, with its charm and its prestige, is the superb head, whence shines the Idea, the French genius, over the world : the haughty head, which lifts itself proudly above all the cities of the earth to fascinate them, to dazzle them, to bid them to her fêtes, to draw them to her pleasures—the foolish head sometimes, not always proof against dizziness. Ten other cities more populous, more picturesque, more opulent than Reims, themselves also famous in history, rival her in energy, and with reason boast that they are more potent centres of national activity ; but not one dreams of disputing with Reims the glory of being the heart of France.

[1] Pastoral Letter of His Eminence Cardinal Mercier, Christmas, 1914.

The Cathedral of Reims

We were reminded of this twenty years ago. France in 1896 celebrated her origin ; she read again with emotion in the first page of her annals the act of her baptism, and she bowed before Reims ; she fell upon her knees in the Cathedral of Reims, for she was born there, on the morrow of that battle of Tolbiac where already, race against race, the Germans disputed the soil with the Franks of Clovis.

France became conscious of herself at Reims ; she found there her characteristic note, her orientation, her ideal. For fourteen centuries she flourished upon the Pact of Reims, which linked her destiny to that of the Church.[1]

Joan of Arc re-established it in the Fourteenth century by bringing about the re-signing at Reims of the original Pact, which was, and remained, the Providential Law of our History. The consecrations at Reims had no other meaning, no other end in view than the taking one by one of the kings of France, and making them, one and all, adhere to the Pact of Reims. Our misfortunes have had no other cause than the rupture of the Pact of Reims at the end of the Eighteenth century. It took more than a hundred years for this attempt at national apostasy to get the better of the robust Christian temperament which France had imbibed in the Baptistery of Reims. But it succeeded in the end, and France, once having strayed from the traditional paths, became a backslider from her mission. The Chosen People refused to serve. But they were carried further than they wished. Without seeing clearly or

---

[1] Mgr. Baudrillart, in his beautiful discourse on the Soul of France at Reims, delivered on the 30th of September, 1914, at St. Clotilde's at Paris, gave to this truth its full meaning and its right historical setting.

104

properly understanding what they were doing, they permitted themselves this evolution, this revolution ; they
would go the whole way ; the Pact of Reims should be
broken, Religion be banished, the State established under a
regime of official Atheism : *Nolumus hunc regnare super nos !*

And Him Whom they thus spurned was no earthly king,
unworthy or blundering, who had ceased to please ; it was
Christ, the friend of the Franks, Who had so loaded them
with gifts that the world had grown jealous.

And so that happened which was bound to happen.
Politics were aggressively employed to vanquish resistance
and reduce opposition. They were applied to driving out
the Church from all its positions, to forcing it back, to
barring its way, to paralysing its action, to disputing its
influence in every direction.

Then came those deplorable conflicts which were even
more full of evil for the country than for the Church ; for
while trials revived the energies of the Church, these
divisions and scandals enervated the country, and gave it
a bad name beyond its borders.

Of what use is silence about it ? How can it be hidden,
since all the world knows it ? It was the sin of France, her
national sin. She must expiate it ; she must repent of it.

But once again, though the head could attempt this
folly, the head alone is not enough when it comes to expiation ; it is the heart which disavows, and expiates, the follies
of the head. That is why Reims has been specially injured
and humiliated :[1] *Cor contritum et humiliatum !*

---

[1] It may be objected that other towns have suffered equally with Reims, and
are also in ruins. But they have been the theatre of fierce combats, have been taken
and retaken, ground to pieces under the infernal artillery of battles. Whereas Reims

That is why Our Lady of Reims has been aimed at. For he who, with secret cunning, determined to deal this blow at France, saw in our Cathedral something besides the joyousness of French art of the Middle Ages, a masterpiece of grace and power, an enchantment for the eyes, a delight for the mind which spread its glory over the city, which radiated its magnificence over the whole country, and which for eight centuries was the marvel of the world ;[1] he saw in it the superb monument of the ancient alliance of 496, the splendid monstrance of the Pact of Reims, our entire past, our history complete, the Baptism and the Coronations, the cradle, the home, the sanctuary of our national life—the most venerable of the Holy Places of France.

It is to that end—mystery of redemption which God has permitted—that all, all of us, have been hurt and humiliated, struck to the heart by the blow which outraged *our* Cathedral—of all of them the most sacred, the most superb, the most triumphant, the best beloved, that within which it seemed that the soul of France was enclosed.

Ah ! truly the blow struck home. France cried out in pain. All of us and each one of us, injured already, and in pain from our own wounds, in spite of so much deep suffer-

has been devastated without being fought over, except in the spring of 1918, when she was already no more than cinders and ruins. The Germans destroyed her methodically, coldly, cynically, stage by stage, without being constrained thereto by any military necessity.

[1] Descriptions of Our Lady of Reims abound. Its worth was known in the old times. The moderns, provoked by the catastrophe, retell, in a tone more profoundly moved, its history, and praise, with still greater love, its marvellous vesture of stone and its mystic soul. Among them I single out with particular pleasure, *La Cathedrale de Reims, A French Work*, by L. Brénier, published by M. Laurens (6, Rue de Tournon, Paris) ; for I do not know of anyone who has treated this subject so adequately and with such mastery.

ing that we were weeping in the secrecy of our homes, and were plunged into the depths of tribulation for our country —all and each one of us have yet mourned this disaster, as one mourns a personal misfortune. Letters from the absent, from friends, from strangers, were watered with tears, like letters of mourning.

The confidences which one receives, the echoes one catches, the conversations one overhears by chance in the street, those pieces of unfinished sentences, which are not addressed to anyone, which spring from the heart with a sigh of anguish or of anger, words of children, reflections of unknown persons, of passers-by who think they are alone—all this astonishes, grips and moves one, so much intense distress does it reveal, sometimes expressed in artless and unlettered phrases.

" I would rather have seen my own house burn ! " How often have I heard that said. The poor sufferers themselves, from the smoking ruins of their own homes, have declared that to see the Cathedral burning hurt them still more. And that was no mere manner of speaking. In the presence of that furnace of thirty-five acres devouring the city, hearts were too broken not to be sincere.

I have taken this heart-cry from a letter from a high-spirited soldier : " I would have given the life of one of my sons—I have six, whom I love tenderly—to save the Cathedral." And this other, which springs with a sob from the heart of a child : " The good God seems to have abandoned France."

And the attitude of the soldiers. Here is an instance.

Some hundreds of them are coming from a distance away in the country. At a turn of the road the Cathedral suddenly appears, on fire. Stunned for a moment, they stop, unable to move, dumb with emotion, a mist of tears in their eyes ; then, as by instinct and as one man, they pull themselves together, come to attention and give the military salute. Is it not strange that the rod with which God has chastised us should be the same race which flung itself upon the Franks of the Fifth century, the descendants of the Germans of Tolbiac, come again to teach us more thoroughly and more clearly the lesson of past happenings ?

Needed thus for this rôle of instruments of justice, they have been able to glorify themselves for a moment over the task which they have performed, over the fierceness with which they have accomplished it, as though they were to reap for themselves all the profit of our misfortunes. But their insolent pride has lasted but for a time ; the expiation once achieved, God has treated them as one treats the stick which one has pulled from the ground in order to inflict a thrashing ; one breaks it and casts it far away with contempt.

When one finds, at the root of every manifestation of German thought, the spirit of Luther, his influence, his note, and remembers that the daughter does not abjure her father ; when one hears the Kaiser speak of " his friend " Luther ; when one reads again his letter to the Princess of Hesse in 1901, on the morrow of her abjuration, one has the right to ask oneself if, on analysing it, one would not discover at the bottom of the Prussian conscience where this sacrilegious crime was elaborated, some leaven of Lutheranism, of the old rancour of the Reformers against the Church and the Blessed Virgin.

It seems, at any rate, that they had a suspicion of this

Pl. 61

Photo Thinot

THE GREAT BREACH OF THE 12TH OF OCTOBER, 1914, AT THE UPPER GALLERY
OF THE APSE (*see pp. 80 and 134; face p. 108*)

Pl. 62

Photo Thinot

THE DECAPITATED ANGEL (11TH NOVEMBER, 1914) AT THE 1ST COUNTERFORT
OF THE APSE (SOUTH SIDE) (*see p.* 135; *face p.* 109)

at Geneva, and that among the Calvinists some embarrassment was felt in consequence. M. Emile Lombard, member of the Consistory, explains it very frankly in the *Journal de Genève* of the 8th of October, 1914.

" As Protestants we are bound to stigmatize vigorously as it deserves an act which offends the Catholic Faith in one of its most noble manifestations, and one most worthy of the human race.

" Truly, that great nation which prides itself upon having inaugurated the Reformation has no cause to be proud of the proofs of superiority which it is giving to the world. Some among us will not be able to listen to the Chorale of Luther without feeling sick, as we think of the kind of exploits which it serves at the moment to celebrate.

" It appears to me to be, just now, urgently necessary to repudiate certain alliances. . . . May the energy of our disavowal underline the fact that there are several forms of Protestantism in the world."

The French Protestants, though not going so far, have written and spoken in the same sense.[1]

But, if the intention is vague, the fact remains, whether they wished it or not, that the wrong they have done reaches also to Our Lady.

When we speak indifferently of " the Cathedral " or of " Notre-Dame " we do not confound the Palace with the Queen ; we affirm that the Palace is the Queen's, and that she is at home there ; we mean to say that the Cathedral is her domain, her sanctuary, that one cannot separate the one from the other, that to touch the Cathedral is to touch

---

[1] See the manifesto of the Council of the Federation of the Protestant Churches in France. (*Le Temps*, 16th October, 1914.)

Our Lady, and to outrage the Cathedral is to outrage Our Lady.

Let us understand this matter.

Apart from the fact that it could not be helped, it was not the presence of the German wounded which profaned Notre-Dame. Willingly, in old times the church and the hospital—the "Hotel Dieu" as one called it—were joined, and on more than one occasion authority was taken from the appeal of Jesus : " Come to Me, all you who suffer " for allowing the hospital to overflow into the church.

The outrage was those sinister sounds which were hurled from beyond the horizon at Our Lady like a roar of blasphemy. It was those formidable blows which insulted her. It was the blood shed in violation of the laws of warfare, that triple crime on the morning of the 18th, and those of the afternoon, which polluted her. It was over there, in the German lines, those jaws of hell, which spat upon the Sanctuary. It was higher and farther away, in the soul of the responsible Master, that sacrilegious *fiat* which had ordered, or had allowed, it to be done !¹

One had but to re-enter the Cathedral the day after in order to receive with emphasis enough this impression of a temple profaned. The eyes which saw it will never forget that vision ; smoking timbers scattered over the Parvis ; a mass of broken stones, each fragment of which incarnated a part of the splendour of the Entrance ; the left tower eaten away, burned, ravaged—the august face

¹ Was not the Kaiser at Von Klück's headquarters near Anizy-le-Chateau, during the battles of Soissons—Crouy—Vrégny (the 8th to the 15th January) ? Did he not go as far as the farm of La Perrière, where the attack was fiercest ? His presence, noted in all the newspapers, was no safeguard for the Cathedral of Soissons, which was heavily bombarded during those days, without the slightest military reason.

Pl. 63

Photo Thinot

SHELL OF THE 12TH NOVEMBER, 1914, IN THE SANCTUARY
(IT ENTERED THROUGH A WINDOW) (*see* p. 135; *face* p. 110)

Pl. 64

Photo Thinot

AN UNEXPLODED SHELL OF THE 17TH OF NOVEMBER, 1914, ON THE ROOF

(see p. 139; face p. 111)

of Our Lady disfigured, like those which have been branded by the horrible scar of a burn ; the three porches which used to shut out the tumult and vulgarity of the street now gaping open ; the windows, through whose pitifully empty frames there now escaped the atmosphere of devotion, the last breath of prayer, and the fading perfume of incense ! From the threshold to the choir rails, and right up to the altar, a thick couch of black cinders. In the naves three half-carbonized corpses, twisted, convulsed with suffering, swollen, tumid, with foam on their lips ! Before the pulpit, by the side of the great broken-down chandeliers, a heap of blankets which the fire had not been able to consume, some formless débris, some soldiers' boots, a caldron, a number of plates and dishes, and soiled chamber utensils ! Farther away the fleshless carcass of a horse. And all this in a heavy, stifling atmosphere, fouled with the odour of burnt cloth and roasted flesh !

See, Mary, into what state they have put your house, what they have done to your Sanctuary : " *incenderunt igni sanctuarium tuum et polluerunt tabernaculum nominis tui !* "[1]

They have forced you to leave it, for they have polluted it. They have chased you from your home !

Hatred cannot enter into your heart : you are the Mother of infinite mercies, and on Calvary you listened while Jesus prayed for his executioners.

But justice is not hate. Sacrilege calls for chastisement. Christ Jesus, avenge Your Mother ! Humble those who have insulted her ! Humble them in their military pride, in their soldiers' savage haughtiness !

[1] Ps. lxxiii. 7.

III

V

THE DISASTER

I

Pl. 65

Photo Thinot

THE BREACH OF THE 22ND NOVEMBER, 1914, IN THE LOWER GALLERY
OF THE CHEVET (see pp. 135 and 140; face p. 114)

Pl. 66

Photo Thinot

CHAPEL OF SAINT NICAISE RUINED BY THE BLAST OF A "210" WHICH FELL IN THE STREET (26TH NOVEMBER, 1914)

(see p. 136; face p. 115)

CHAPTER V

THE DISASTER

WHEN the telegraph sent forth to the four corners of the earth the stupefying news, "They have set fire to the Cathedral of Reims," journalists did not wait for the extinguishment of the fire before measuring its extent ; and, in the bewilderment of the first moments, they put things at their worst. Their feverish pens, which travel too quickly, often travel too far.

No ; there remains of the Cathedral something besides a mass of cinders and a pile of ruins.

To us others, to us who know and mourn, when it happens on certain misty days that we approach the Cathedral by way of the Place du Parvis, there comes upon us the impression of escape from the nightmare ; each time we get the illusion that it is still there, sovereignly beautiful, as in the old time. To see it thus, from the front, one would swear that it has not suffered the least deformation in its great architectural lines (Plate 19).

Let those come, then, who have not had the consolation of not having seen it before its misfortune : let them come to it when the daylight is fading, at the hour when the noises of the street are softened in the evening stillness, or yet later, if the moon, in the mysterious silence of the night, envelops it in that dream-light which spiritualizes and transfigures it ; let them stop, keep silence, and gaze, the while their eyes drink in that splendid vision of beauty ; and let them then go away without proceeding farther. For with a few paces more the illusion would vanish brutally (Plate 20).

As soon as one advances the wounds which disfigure the Entrance disclose themselves plainly, and the sight is heartrending ; and directly one moves to one side or the other, the disaster shows itself, immense, indescribable— so great that in simply returning to-day to the inventory which we took on that 4th of September, there comes over me a grief-laden anxiety, like that of those who, on the battle-field, when the fighting is over, approach a wounded man, torn by shell-fire ; they hesitate, they feel a sense of dread ; they do not know what to do or where to begin.

That north tower, which had been clutched and blackened and flared over three stories by the falling scaffolds, bitten in its vitals by the fire, nearly half of the marvellous façade, that amazing page of sculpture, a very world of statues, so beautifully arranged, so harmonious, with all its exuberance, the triumphal escort of Our Lady : all that is ravaged ! (Plate 21).

On the ground, among the charred beams, blocks from the two fallen pinnacles ; to the right and left of the great double bay, fragments of columns, débris of sculpture, pieces of statues, scraps of drapery and lace, flowers and torn foliage, *chefs-d'œuvre* in atoms ! (Plate 22).

One wants to gather up these fragments one by one, and put them back in their place ; for the eye seeks, and finds, the points where they were torn away, the breakages and the mutilations.

But, from top to bottom of this immense façade, but

116

Pl. 67

Photo Poirier

SHELL OF THE 21ST FEBRUARY, 1915, THE FIRST WHICH PIERCED THE CEILING

(see pp. 137 and 169; face p. 116)

Pl. 68

SHELL OF THE 26TH FEBRUARY, 1915, WHICH BROKE DOWN THE WALL
UNDER A WINDOW IN THE NORTH TRANSEPT (see p. 138)

SHELL OF THE 25TH OF MARCH, 1915, AT THE ANGLE AT THE BASE OF THE
GABLE (NORTH TRANSEPT) (see p. 138; face p. 117)

yesterday chiselled and worked like the precious panel of a reliquary, the charred stone is crumbling, and rising in flakes which will fall to-morrow.

The great statues which back against the embrasures of the porch, the disfigurement of which we deplored on the 4th of September, are now in a pitiable condition (Plate 23). The Queen of Saba, that gracious figure at the point of the counterfort, is horribly mutilated ; a decapitated bust[1] and one arm ! The rest has no longer a human form (Plate 24).

At the returning angle her neighbour, St. Sixtus, has preserved only his head upon a body which looks as though it had been hammered. The other personages on this side are only half demolished. In front, the Angel who smiled at St. Nicaise the martyr—" the smile of Reims "—has no longer his arms ; his head has rolled to the ground (Plate 25). One still recognizes St. Clotilde, also hammered, and scraped from the shoulders to the feet ; but St. Rémi and St. Thierry are no more than frightful mummies, corpses enveloped in a winding sheet, the contours of which one can scarcely divine (Plate 26).

The pedestals and the dais, the lintel, the tympan, the covings, the arch at the side, are riddled with injuries (Plate 27).

The Crucifixion group, above the porch, hardly exist any more. The seven personages are scorched from head to foot. Christ has the face flattened and crushed ; the left arm has disappeared ; the centurion has neither arm nor head ; there is not one which is not mutilated (Plate 28).

---

[1] The head has since been recovered, in a good condition. The Abbé Thinot had found it, and put it in a place of safety.

There is no longer any trace of the delicate bell-turrets which emerged at the point where the gables met. The gargoyles which projected a little lower down are broken (Plate 29). Of the musician seated above—David, I believe —there remains only the legs, with half of the harp between the knees. The caryatides, sheltered by the heads of monsters, have just been saved. Still lower, the symbolic personages who represent the rivers of Paradise are seriously damaged.

The ravishing scene of the coronation of the Virgin, in its sumptuous framing, worked in the style of antique ivory, is destroyed (Plate 28), with the Great Rose, and the Gallery of the Gloria, on its left side entirely ; a big vertical line, in the axis of the Entrance, marks off clearly the zone of destruction ; the scaffolding stopped there.

On the higher story, just beneath the Baptism of Clovis, the history of David is displayed. Was he not the first king anointed by Samuel, as Clovis was at Reims by St. Rémi ? His fight with Goliath is depicted in two scenes— the blow with the sling, and the blow with the sabre. In the angle, at the right foot of the coving, he appears again, as the ancestor of Our Lady, in company with Solomon ;[1] all this statuary is destroyed, to the left of the middle line. Above, the balustrade of the Gallery of Kings, with its angels, is thrown down (Plate 30) ; the dead Goliath is only a shape-less mass, and the little David suggests his great act with the stumps of arms. In the arch framing the Rose window

---

[1] The identification of these two beautiful statues, with their wonderful vigour of expression, has provoked a good deal of discussion. We should perhaps recognize, in the statue on the right, St. James of Compostella, to whom our French kings had a special devotion, and, in that on the left, booted and with a more modern manner, a member of the Reims Brotherhood of Pilgrims of Compostella. (See L. Bréhier, *La Cathedrale de Reims*, p. 125.)

the small figures which recall other episodes in his life have vanished.

In the two uncrowned pinnacles, in front of the tower, and in the two others behind, in the Rue Robert de Coucy, the great statues (they measure four metres), of Christ as pilgrim, of St. John, and of Christ risen showing His wounds to St. Thomas, resemble blocks of badly quarried stone ; only the heads, which are more under the niches, have been protected (Plate 21).

The central porch has suffered little relatively. For a long time we thought that it had no other injuries than five or six wide rents in the vestments of the figures in the group of the Presentation, and some serious gashes in the covings ; the worst of all was not revealed until later.

Licked and bitten by the fire which devoured the enormous door which it supports, exposed to the heat of the immense furnace which was formed by the piling up of wood from the scaffolding, the Virgin on the pier was in the midst of the furnace. She seemed not to have been touched ; in reality she was burned. She is cracking, and there is reason to fear that she will entirely fall to pieces.

It pulls at the heart strings when one penetrates into the Cathedral, more even than on going into a house where some one is lying dead, because to the dull impression of desolation and mourning there is added the overwhelming sensation evoked by the crime and the profanation.

If one followed one's inclination, one would remain there, saying nothing, just looking, praying, weeping : *illic sedimus et flevimus*.[1]   But there is imposed upon us to-day

[1] Ps. cxxxvi.

the painful task of exploring this Calvary ; the sad pilgrimage must be pursued.

The naves are now cleared ; the corpses are no longer there ; the cinders, the rubbish, the ignoble waste matter from the ambulance has been taken away ; the Cathedral appears an immense void (Plate 31).

It is no longer the cloistral solitude, peaceful and warm, of the sanctuary ; it is the desert, and the abnormal desert which devastation has made sinister.

M. Thinot and I returned later, one sombre winter's night. The wind raged above ; it rushed in squalls along the naves, through the open windows, with the noise of a hurricane in the great forests. One would have said that the maleficent Powers of the shades were taking violent possession of the Temple which the maleficence of man had polluted.

Foolish doors, half in cinders, banged in the high galleries; débris of windows torn from their frames fell upon the stones with a clear noise ; and rubbish detached from the arches dropped with a dull sound upon the floor.

Groping along we gained the altar of the Holy Virgin ; and on our knees in silence we wept.

Instinctively, upon entering, the eyes uneasily search the roof, as though surprised at not seeing the sky appearing through a hole or some wide breaches ; then rapidly they scrutinize the naves, the sanctuary, right along to the farthest point, astonished to find that not a single pillar is thrown down, not a wall pierced. Were it not indeed for the miserable condition of the windows, and of those blackened and burnt stones at the base of the pillars

(Plate 32), one would hardly believe, now that the church has been cleared, that it had been the theatre of such tragic scenes.

Quite otherwise is the impression as soon as one turns round. Whereas the straw was spread in the naves, a pile of it was accumulated near the doors ; and there was in truth a conflagration there. The walls at this spot are injured as badly as on the exterior. The staircases of the towers served as chimneys ; and the traces of the flames may here be seen at a great height. The woodwork of the lobbies, by the lower doors, were caught by the flames, and the fire devastated inestimable pieces of sculpture.

The luxuriant ornamentation which encloses the arch of the three porches, on the reverse of the façade, is peculiar to Reims ; it has its equal nowhere else. The elegant arrangement of those trilobate niches—there are fifty-six in the Great Entrance—which spring out in high relief from a graceful background of foliage, and of the fine statues, with supple figures and easy carriage, full of life, produces the effect of an immense grey tapestry, of very sober design, connecting without effort with the rich tapestries of the lower naves : " this cloth is of the same age as that stone."

It is a miracle that the central panel, the most beautiful of them, which contains pieces of the first order, such as the Crusaders' Communion, has not received a scratch. Of the two others, which were little known, hidden as they were by the unfortunate woodwork, there remains nothing but one or two subjects, and here and there several less remarkable heads which had a pensive appearance in their retirement at the back of the niches ; but even these were, for the most part, so tottering that it was necessary to take them away or they would have toppled over (Plates 33 and 34).

The great tapestries of the Sixteenth century, the sumptuous attire of Our Lady, had been sent to Paris on the 3rd of September in a long convoy of precious objects which the Government despatched to the south, in order to preserve our artistic treasures from the rapacity of the vandals who confound theft with conquest, and who were sacking Belgium.

If only it could have removed our Thirteenth-century glass also ! The most ancient windows, those in the apse, at least the three in the middle, are only slightly touched. Four others, behind the transept, two on each side, are riddled with holes ; the last are in shreds.

Of the high windows in the nave, whose colouring of reds, purples, and intense blues is so amazingly warm and vigorous, which burnished the rays of the midday sun, only one, out of twenty, is intact ;[1] six are still almost entire. Some of them I see literally riddled, four three-parts gone, and two completely empty of glass (Plates 35 and 36).

As for that marvel, the Great Rose of the Entrance, that dazzling mosaic of flowers, where shine in glory around Our Lady triumphant all the fires of the rainbow, it is broken through the middle ; half of it remains (Plate 37).

The illuminated gallery of the triforium, of a more severe tone, which formed a kind of modulated foundation of light for the Rose window has, with it, suffered the effects of the fire ; the four bays in the right have flown into pieces ; it has suffered, in addition, from the fall of stones. Though

[1] The first in the choir, beyond the transept on the left.

one or two bays on the left still preserve some panels entire, the others only retain some beautiful fragments hanging by a thread from the ironwork.

One only of the two roses in the transept, that at the northern cross-bar, belongs to the Thirteenth century ; it is very badly damaged—less, however, than the other, which had been altogether destroyed by a storm and restored in the Sixteenth century.

Among the high windows in the transept are some remarkable antique grisailles, dishonoured by a hideous coat of stone colour ; the first, at the south-west angle, which was cleaned recently, has a very fine effect, and is in perfect condition.

The windows on the floor level, despoiled of their old Eighteenth-century glasses, had no longer any artistic interest. They are empty of glass, full of holes, or broken in.

The Little Rose of the Entrance, without value or character, which the plans for the restoration had condemned, and which has now disappeared, is no matter for regret.

In the great modern window above the sacristies, one counts several holes. The sombre windows of a blue (perhaps too monotonous) tone in the Chapel of the Blessed Sacrament, and those of a sweet pearly tint in the Sacred Heart Chapel, were seriously spattered by the fall of a shell in the street, by the apse, and the pressure of air, forcing the glass away from the lead, has left an empty silhouette of some of the figures.

There is no damage in the sacristies beyond the demolition by a shell of the stone staircase which descends from the Hall of the Kings to the crypt.

The artistic furnishing of the transept, which we had had no time to save, the two Gobelin tapestries, the canvasses of Titian, Tintoret, Nicolas Poussin, Zuccharo, and Mutiano, the picture of J. Tissot and the others, have not received the slightest scratch.

The great lustre in the Chapel of the Blessed Sacrament fell three days after the fire (Plate 38).

A cloth still hanging from the communion table in the Cardinal's chapel, is covered with lead. Here, in big drops, fallen from the ceiling, they have splashed down upon it like tears ; there, little drops have powdered it with a fine dust, which have congealed on it without burning the cloth (Plate 39).

The delicate and precious Joan of Arc by P. d'Epinay, behind the choir,[1] has been preserved complete, as has that of P. Dubois on the Parvis.

The fire swept the choir up to the altar, for the chairs had been piled up here ; but it did not go farther.

The stalls on the left have been completely consumed (Plate 40). M. Andrieux was just able to save those on the right, in addition to the Archbishop's throne, which the fire had already touched.

The pavement of the sanctuary has been lifted up in places ; the marble stones have split, and the rents in them made me think of the rich coronation carpet, that other splendour, which displayed on great feast days, upon a purple ground, the arms of France at the foot of the altar, and which has perished (Plate 40).

The organ had already got into such a dilapidated

---

[1] This statue, deposited at the Cathedral in 1909, is the property of M. H. Abelé, of Reims.

Pl. 69

SHELL OF THE 21ST MARCH, 1915, AT THE CHEVET

Photos Poirier

THE SAME BREACH, SEEN FROM THE INTERIOR (*see p. 138; face p. 124*)

Pl. 70

Photo Sainsaulieu

PIER OF A COUNTERFORT (AT THE CHEVET), INJURED AND LOOSENED,

8TH APRIL, 1915 (*see p. 139; face p. 125*)

condition that private generosity had provided for its complete restoration. The bombardment has shaken it to such an extent that one can no longer draw a sound from it. It will be resuscitated with the Cathedral.[1]

At the north entrance only some notches have been made ; nothing of importance is destroyed ; three or four splinterings on the mouth of the statue of our Lord ; one on the pedestal ; another in the devil's stomach, near the hell caldron by the tympan (Plate 41) ; yet another in the ceiling. At the other door I found only two : in the tunic of King Clovis, on the right side, and one in the tympan at the end of the third fillet.

We mount by the truncated towers of the transept ; and, high up, before arriving at the gallery of the Prophets, we discover a loophole which the architect had not provided for. It is a big hole, opening in the direction of the belfry of St. Andrew ; a shell has pierced the tower.

A couple of paces, and we are in full view of the disaster. So often had we made this pilgrimage that we had become familiarized with the desolation of these ruins. One does not accustom oneself to it, but the eyes, little by little, become so, and the shock is less violent.

On this day, in coming out suddenly, through the little door which pierces the gable end in that narrow enclosure without horizon, cut in the centre by strange arches, like bridges thrown across a ravine ; at the appearance of this immense skeleton partly buried under cinders ; at the

---

[1] This magnificent gift was offered to Our Lady of Reims by the Countess Werlé. The plans are ready, and the house of Cavallié-Coll is only awaiting the resumption of worship to proceed with the work.

sight of the naked reins of the vaults amid this dismal environment of catastrophe, the blow was violent and grievous, as
on the morrow of the fire when we re-entered the church
(Plate 42). That nevertheless was somehow different—less
profound, and less keen. There is not now, in the same
degree, that pressure upon the soul which then crushed so
hardly upon us, but rather a sensation of anguish at heart,
mingled with anger and fury, a sort of shame also that men
should have done this thing.

We looked without being able to speak, for at first we
felt bewildered : one needed time to take it in, to orientate
oneself, to recollect oneself ; and then we felt that any
words we could utter would be too inadequate and too
cold ; we hesitated, lest we might profane, by a banality, a
sadness so profound. It needed an effort to recover oneself,
to recover the connection between this fantastic wreckage
and the realities which had disappeared (Plate 43).

There was not the smallest vestige of the woodwork ;
it has been consumed to the last brand (Plate 44). The
cinders accumulated in the space between the roof and
ceilings are almost white. The centres of the *oculi*, at the
keys of the vaulting, stand out in alignment on the extrados ;
one would take them for the kerbing round wells.

The eye seeks points of guidance. The gables of the
transept and that of the façade between the towers show
the line of the roof (Plate 45). Those robust arches, supported on the big pillars of the transept, which served as
the base of the great central steeple which was destroyed
in the Fifteenth century, and never rebuilt, carried the
carillon (Plate 46) ; a confused mass of twisted iron, of
indented clock wheels, of broken and melted bells, marks

Pl. 71

Photo Sainsaulieu

NORTH TOWER (REAR VIEW)
THREE BREACHES: ON THE RIGHT, 22ND FEBRUARY, 1915; ON THE LEFT,
1ST JUNE, 1915; ON THE TOP, 15TH JUNE, 1915 (*see p. 140; face p. 126*)

Pl. 72

BREACH IN THE UPPER GALLERY (SOUTH SIDE) NEAR THE TOWER

(SHELL OF 15TH JUNE, 1915) *(see p. 140; face p. 127)*

the spot where it had been (Plate 47); it has fallen over also on the side of the Archbishop's Palace.

As for that little masterpiece of woodwork and lead which we called "the Angel's belfry," so elegant with its octagonal balcony and its curious caryatides of beaten lead, types and costumes of the Fifteenth century, with its steeple so slenderly worked in fleurs-de-lis, that was broken in two in its fall. From the midst of the debris of ironwork we picked up some pieces of the ancient bell which was daily sounded at the Elevation at the chapter Mass, in virtue of a foundation of the Sixteenth century, and which was called "the bell of the Blessed Sacrament" (Plate 48); but the top of the belfry, the copper boule and the shaft which ran through the angel weather vane have been thrown down to the lower story, upon the chapels in the apse, in the angle of the transept (Plate 49).

At no place better than here, in the extrados of the great roof, can one obtain an idea of the ravages of the fire, for taking its measure and appreciating its extent. A heart-rending spectacle of devastation, striking the beholder with consternation, revolting him, as he thinks of what those cinders were made, and how, and by whom. And this suffering becomes exasperated upon analysis, for the evil stands self-confessed at each step, and each detail underlines its importance.

Everywhere the stone is profoundly disturbed and torn apart in the nave and in the aisles; everywhere it lies loose and chipped. The heavy stones of the *chemin de ronde*, though they were not in immediate contact with the fire, are cracked; they come apart under one's feet, as soon as one advances a little on the edge. And, when one looks closer, one sees that in certain parts, which seem to have been spared, the stone has been (as they say) " astonished," and that one day it will give way (Plate 50).

In the apse some chapels—six of them—have preserved their leaden roofs.[1]   On the 20th of September the fire had caught in this region ; we were able to arrest it, and save nearly all which had not been burned the day before.

It is astonishing that the ceilings did not give way at any point under the battering of shells or under the weight of the enormous mass of fallen timber.   Strongly supported by the flying buttresses, they resisted.   The robust skeleton of the building has not yielded.

On all sides we find traces of the bombardment.   But how many others have been effaced by the fire ?   All those gaping wounds in the roof, with their lead gone, curled back violently by the currents of air made by the explosions, all that has disappeared ; and there is here a gap in our calculations.   The Abbé Thinot who, from day to day, registered each new fall, was not able on the Saturday to make his tour of inspection, and it is likely that several injuries have escaped him.

If, from below, on the Place, the towers give an illusion, here one sees the actual position; the upper part of the north tower is seriously dislocated (Plate 51); the spring of the spire is pierced behind ; the heavy stone bases have slid and been pushed out.   At the summit of the turret on the right the enormous slab which covers the opening has been loosened, lifted, and put out of position by the blast of a shell (Plate 52).

One of the rear axles on the south tower is pierced, in the direction of the Place Royale (Plate 53).

[1] Beginning at the north transept, as far as the sixth counterfort.

The top gallery of the great nave has been broken at one point, and that of the apse in two places, by shells which penetrated the roof.

On the lower story, at the angle of the north cross-bar and the chevet, we count four shells : the first broke the spring of the flying buttress, the pieces of which staved in the roofs of the chapels (Plates 54 and 55) ; the second pulverized the tiles covering the truncated tower ; the two others struck the great bays on the first stage ; the stone has been crushed and pounded, and a little column in the lower gallery has flown off ; the fragments which shattered the window have also inside the church broken the wood-work of the great organ and chipped a capital in the transept.

On the same side still, but higher up, a gargoyle is broken, and an eagle has been decapitated.

A flying buttress in the apse, the second on the south side, has been hit at the coping of the lower spring of the flying buttress ; on one side there is a big contusion ; on the other a wide and deep cut, though the arch has not been broken. The neighbouring window has been slashed, as though with a whip ; the gargoyle above the last counter-fort has been broken (Plate 56).

In the courtyard of the Archbishop's palace the pinnacle of the fifth buttress has been cut off in the middle (Plate 57) ; complete layers of the pyramid have been projected in a single piece upon the roofs of the lower nave. The pillar of the third has been struck full in the thick part of the masonry. Fragments of this shell sent the stone tracery flying, as well as the framework of the rose in the neighbouring window ; they also killed several of the wounded.

Gazing along the tracery of stone arches, in the upper

parts of the edifice, we discover, at the angle of the transept, a gargoyle drowned in lead, wearing a fantastic aspect. It has on the back a great coat of armour of it, a cope whose fringes hang over its flanks ; it vomits from its open mouth a rigid stream of it, which elongates and tapers out into a stalactite ; and beneath it wide seams fixed to the stone projections descend in a cascade to the foot of the gallery (Plate 58).

In order to gain the north tower, and continue our exploration, we traverse the façade on the outside, on the level of the triforium, behind the gables of the three porches.

Starting from the middle, we have to pick our way over the heap of rubbish where lie pell-mell among great stones fallen from the gallery and the pinnacles, important pieces of architecture and delicate fragments of ornamentation, the accumulation of which makes an affecting sight.

As far as the first counterfort on the Rue Robert de Coucy the breaking away and falling of beams have made the same ravages as the fire. The pinnacle of this counterfort has been decrowned ; at one of the bell-turrets the great chain of the winch has come off, and remains hanging.

The pigeons of Notre-Dame, unfortunate victims plunged into bewilderment and driven away by the catastrophe, have given up to quarrelsome crows their comfortable shelters in the holes in the walls, under the high cornices ; they have sought, lower down, quieter nooks in the shadow of the covings, in the towers and in the solitary walks on the stairways. Our going up disturbed them ; they flew off noisily from beneath our feet.

We had thought that the bells had fallen in with the belfry, but we were not expecting what we actually saw.

Pl. 73

Photo Sainsaulieu

SHELL OF 21ST JULY, 1915, IN THE APSE (CHAPEL OF ST. CÉLINIE),
WINDOW BLOWN AWAY AND BUTTRESS INJURED (see p. 141; face p. 130)

Pl. 74

Photo Sainsaulieu

SHELL OF 21ST JULY, 1915; BREACH IN THE LOWER GALLERY OF THE CHEVET
(see p. 141; face p. 131)

The Disaster

We possessed eight beautiful bells, which rang a full peal. A long time ago, in order to lighten the belfry, which was in a bad state, five of them were taken down. They are still there, lying in a row. The biggest and lowest toned bell, which used to ring the Angelus, has received a blow; it is cracked and unusable. The second, Stéphanie, which used to ring the curfew, is intact, as also are the two smallest; but the three which fell from the cage into the furnace were literally melted, one altogether, another half-melted, while the third, which fell a little to the side, had begun to lose shape and fall in (Plate 59).

I look at these corpses of bells with eyes which see further, which search for something else. It is of the bourdons, the great bells, that I am thinking. I hasten to satisfy myself.

One stage more, the last ! What will it show us ?

I go in advance of my companions. I mount slowly with a feeling of oppression at the heart, and with the mind tense, ready for anything. At the outlet of the narrow passage which leads to the bourdons instinctively I lean over towards the abyss where doubtless they are lying with the other bells; there is no abyss, not the least trace of fire, but the solid floor from which emerge the massive beams of the belfry. I lift up my head and see at their post, proud and tranquil, our two bourdons, " the solemn voices of Our Lady "—the voices of the great days when Providence permitted us to celebrate, after the *Te Deum* of victory, the glorious restoration of Patriotism and the Faith.[1]

[1] On Monday the 11th November, 1918, in honour of the signing of the armistice the bells were rung, associating the war's Great Wounded thing and the martyr city with the joys of victory.

The Cathedral of Reims

Such was the state of the Cathedral on the morrow of the fire. It had received, according to our reckoning, forty-two shells which we had noted, and this figure is certainly a minimum. Since then they have not spared it much ; that is the least that one can say. On several occasions they have aimed at it. It received between the 24th September, 1914, and the 5th October, 1918, 245 shells, without counting the storm of the 24th April, 1917, which it has not been possible to calculate, nor the spring of 1918[1] (21st of March to 25th June) ; for they treated the Cathedral as they treated the city, as a hostage ; and each time that at some point or other of the front they received a check, a disappointment, or something which vexed them, they struck it. This happened with such regularity that in advance, as one feels a storm coming, we knew of the approach of their blows.[2]

[1] See Appendix C. List of shells which struck the Cathedral.

[2] We could have no doubt about that ; but it needed the *débâcle* of 1918 to furnish us with the palpable proof—the following telephone message found in the archives of a German battery, on the Reims front.

" Kommandantur of Field Artillery,
　　　Br. B. No. 584/17.
Telephone message No. 476 of 6/6/17.
The group will in future reply to the fire of the enemy artillery directed against the depot of the forest house by immediate reprisal shots on Reims Cathedral.
The battery of the 4th D.O. (1st Res. 9th) will be charged to undertake this reprisal firing.
The opening of fire will be ordered on each occasion by the E. M. of the 4th D. I
　　　　　　　　　　　　　　　　　　NEITZEL.
　　　　　　　　　　　(*Le Matin*, 9th March, 1919)."

And, as they must always add hypocrisy to their ill-doing, they still dare after that, after all that they have done, to publish, among themselves and among neutrals, postcards in which Our Lady of Reims, in the midst of the ruined town, rises intact, and with this inscription surrounding the top of the towers : " *Den Deutschen ein Heiligthum !*—A thing sacred to the Germans ! "

Pl. 75

THE NAVES INUNDATED BY RAIN *(see p. 144; face p. 132)*

Pl. 76

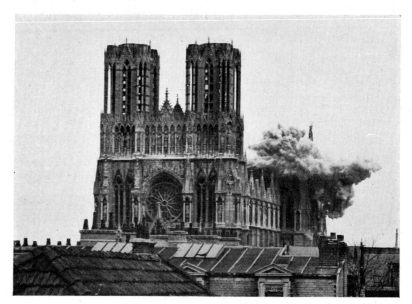

Photos Glorget

EXPLOSIONS OF "340's" (APRIL 1917) (*see p*. 146; *face p*. 133)

But the work of destruction was no longer connected with any sensational event.

The dull solitude which was spread like a shroud over the city seems to be still more oppressive in the approaches to the Cathedral. Since the catastrophe life has left this region. Grass has grown up between the paving stones on the Place. One no longer walks along the deserted Parvis, save out of respect ; one only comes here as for a " pilgrimage." The church is shut, and may not be used for religious services (Plate 60). Only the rare footsteps of stranger pilgrims, the moaning of the wind, and the occasional cries of birds, trouble the gloomy silence of the desolated naves.

Time passes there noiselessly, with the monotony of sad days, without any notable thing happening which could be remembered in the history of the Cathedral ; never anything more to note than wounds, injuries, ruins.

It was simply the " pleasure of hurting "—that *Schaden-freude* which is native to Germany[1]—which pointed the guns.

[1] " If the German word *Schadenfreude* (the joy of hurting) has no equivalent in other languages, that is not the simple result of chance. It goes without saying that this trait of character is also to be found more or less pronounced among individuals in other countries ; but then it only appears as the mark of an exceptional moral condition, or a momentary impulse. The German is afflicted with a natural and chronic *Schadenfreude.*"

It is a German who thus speaks of his compatriots—Curt Wigand, in his book *Unkultur* (Berlin, 1905). See the *Revue des Deux Mondes*, 15th September, 1914.

In March, 1917, at the time of the retreat on the Somme, when German ignominy displayed itself more cynically than ever, one comes across this evil kind of joy in their press. The *Berliner Tageblatt*, after a description minute, complaisant and almost jocose, of the awful devastations which had made a desert of this region, closes its article with this agreeable piece of humour : " Poor devil of inhabitant, seek now for your home." They applaud themselves for having such a genius for inflicting injury. The *Vossische Zeitung* writes : " To us it comes as a wave of joy before the

The shots succeeded each other, without military reason, without any motive whatever.

The dates have been noted and the places marked. Up to his departure for the Army (on the 15th of January, 1915) M. Thinot kept count of them. After him I continued the circumstantial account, which unfortunately has the style and the dryness of a *procès-verbal*.

Thursday, 24th of September.—A "150" on the roof, at the inner angle of the north transept and the nave, at the foot of the great arch of the window; one on the north tower; one on the pier of the first counterfort (south side) above the second glacis.

Monday, 12th October.—A "210" knocks down, over a length of four metres, the upper gallery of the chevet, dislocating the neighbouring arcatures (two metres at least on each side). If they are not dragged down, some day or other, by their own weight, these pieces, loose and out of the perpendicular, ready to fall, will come down, at the slightest shaking, upon the lower roofs, and rip open the lead roofing of the small chapels (Plate 61).

It is an enormous breach as one sees it from the Place Royale. (This same day Notre-Dame of Paris received a bomb from a Taube.)

Wednesday, 4th of November.—Grass is growing in the great nave, around the black stone which marks the place of martyrdom of St. Nicaise.

Wednesday, 11th November.—A shell strikes the angel of the first counterfort of the apse, beyond the south cross-

evil which has been done elsewhere." In July, 1918, the *Berliner Tageblatt* again writes, in notifying " the total destruction of a new corner of France; at night one can watch the fires which ravage cornfields and forests. It is a *consoling spectacle*." (Quoted in *La Croix* of the 1st of August, 1918.)

bar ; a column of the niche has been struck ; the angel is still standing, but the head is broken off, and the bust is ruined ; there is only one wing (Plate 62). A bomb which fell on the Parvis has thrown down the barriers which shut off the three doors of the great Entrance, and has added several injuries to those already made in the façade.

Thursday, 12th November.—A " 77 " enters through a window in the apse and explodes on the floor of the sanctuary, near the altar, on the right. It is the first to penetrate the Cathedral. The marble pavements, broken into pieces, have been scattered all around. The Angel in prayer, on the credence, a metre's distance from the place where the blow struck, has not been touched (Plate 63).

Tuesday, 17th November.—A " 150 " falls on the roof, makes a deep break in the corner of one of the great arches of the croisée, and recoils without exploding between two small arches in the great nave (Plate 64).

(The same day the apsidal chapel of St. Rémi is broken in ; the roof and ceiling fall on the altar ; the statue of Notre-Dame de L'Usine, thrown upon the pavement, in the middle of a lot of rubbish, is intact ; the precious glass is destroyed.)

Sunday, 22nd November.—A " 130 " cuts down two small columns in the lower balustrade of the chevet, with their capitals, between the third and fourth buttresses (south side) beneath the first series of animals reconstituted by Viollet-le-Duc (Plate 65). Another, of large calibre, crashes upon a bare wall parallel to the nave at the top of the truncated tower of the north transept (west side).

Monday, 23rd November.—The lower spring of the third counterfort of the nave (south side) struck by shrapnel ;

135

the stone did not fall, but the window was riddled by the iron splinters. Another made a deep gash at the base of the gable end of the north cross-bar on the side of the apse ; pieces of architecture were thrown down, among others a grotesque nun's head, by the bell turret of the pinnacle. A third fell at the foot of the wall of the sacristy of the Treasure, and broke all the windows.

Tuesday, 24*th November*.—A shell bursts up above at the last course but one of the steeple, at the south-west axle of the bourdon tower.

Thursday, 26*th November*.—A " 210 " makes a hole in the path and the wall of the Hôtel du Commerce, covers with white spots the entire side of the Cathedral, and breaks up four windows ; that of the Chapel of the Blessed Virgin is dislocated, torn up, and slashed ; the three windows of the chapel of St. Nicaise, opposite, has been emptied ; nothing remains of them. The overthrown shrine of the saint has rolled to the ground and up to the foot of the altar, with the cross and candlesticks, beneath tangled lumps of leadwork. The columns and the capitals of the baldachino are damaged (Plate 66). A shrapnel shell explodes on the dripstone of the upper gallery of the nave (south side) above the eighth window ; one of the little gargoyles between the counterforts is broken down ; the neighbouring caryatid has one leg and one hand amputated. A " 210 " explodes at the corner of the Entrance, facing the Lion d'Or ; it splashes statues and draperies by the right porch, and has made some ravages on the left side of the central porch. At the last step of the little staircase which unites the Gallery of the Prophets with the truncated tower of the south cross-bar (by the side of the apse) a " 77 " has buried itself in the masonry, and exploded within it. Finally, this same day a shell of very large calibre explodes two paces from Joan of Arc, on the Parvis, without touching her ; it digs a veritable ditch at her feet, breaks and disperses far off on the pavement, and showers shot all over the place ; but Joan of Arc has not a scratch.

Saturday, 28th November.—A shell at the spring of the upper flying buttress of the first counterfort of the nave (south side) ; a breach is made, but the arch is not broken. A " 77 " at the gable of the Assumption (south transept) knocks down the point of the bell turret on the right ; the splinters have riddled the rampart of the gable.

Friday, 4th December.—The bell tower is again struck, on the top, in the rear.

1915. *Thursday, 18th February.*—A shell breaks violently against the second counterfort on the reverse of the north tower, half-way up. Another has struck the chapel of the Archbishop's Palace at the upper part of a counterfort, on the side overlooking the garden.

Sunday, 21st February.—(A very bad night, three thousand shells on the city). A " 150 " bursts on the roof over the sanctuary, near the *oculus ;* the hole is about a couple of hands' breadth (Plate 67). Another breaks off the cornice of the first counterfort of the apse (south side) which had already been struck on the 11th November, and the angel on which was mutilated. A third strikes again the base of the great bay of the truncated tower, in the north transept (by the side of the apse). A fourth has crushed the base of the upper gallery of the nave, between the fourth and fifth counterforts (north side) ; two of the little columns on the small pillars are broken, but the arcature has not given way ; the neighbouring gargoyle—a fine ape's head—has been struck. A fifth has demolished an arcature of the same gallery, between the second and third counterforts. A shrapnel shell, the pieces of which we collected, has burst on the bell tower. Finally, a big splinter coming from a shell which fell in the Rue Robert de Coucy right against the grating at the foot of the tower, has broken in the little blocked-up door which faces the Rue du Trésor.

Monday, *22nd February*.—Three shells at least on the north tower ; two on the summit accentuate the very grave breach already made in the rear ; the other has badly notched, also in the rear, a little column of the turret on the right, that which attaches it to the tower.

Friday, *26th February*.—A shell of very large calibre penetrates through the rosace of the north transept, and knocks down a mass of masonry at the base of the window to the left of the great organ (severe damage) (Plate 68). A shrapnel shell breaks, in three places, the delicate columns of a turret behind the south tower.

Tuesday, *2nd March*.—A " 150 " rips up to a great depth the base of the gable of the Annunciation (north transept) at the right angles : the splinters are embedded in the corner of the gallery under big blocks of stone (Plate 68).

Thursday, *18th March*.—The police report notes two shells on the Cathedral, the striking points of which I have not been able to determine.

Wednesday, *24th March*.—A shrapnel shell breaks down the lead roof of the Chapel of the Blessed Sacrament, and tears to shreds the wood of the ceiling, and bursts under the arching, without piercing it (Plate 69).

Thursday, *8th April*.—(A very bad night ; two thousand shells on the city.) A shell of big calibre loosens and separates the stones of the entire base of a counterfort, at the end of the apse, in the great flagged channel, and so loosens on this side the circumference of the edifice (Plate 70). Another in the courtyard behind, near the sacristies, lays bare the foundations of the chapel of the Archbishop's palace, and ravages all the windows of the chapels of the Rosary and of St. Rémi. A third, a " 210," smashes an arcature in the upper gallery of the nave (south side) opposite the sixth counterfort, breaks the gargoyle underneath, chips the pyramid of the fifth counterfort, strikes a column at the niche of the fourth, cuts off the branch of a tree in the yard, ploughs up the earth for over a metre, and rebounds, without bursting, into the Hôtel du Lion d'Or (Plate 57).

Saturday, *8th May*.—(Traditional feast day of Joan of Arc at Orleans.) Three shrapnel shells on the Parvis, about half-past eleven. The Germans thought no doubt that Reims was keeping the festival of Joan of Arc to-day. The place, which was deserted, would at that hour have been invaded by a crowd coming away from the singing of the Office.

Thursday, *20th May*.—M. Charles Legendre, of Reims, relieves the Cathedral of the " 150 " shell which since the 17th November has slept slyly over the great nave (Plate 64). With fine courage he lifted it up, let it down through the *oculus* of a keystone of a vault, carried it off, dismounted it, emptied it, and deposited it, like a document, in the Treasury of the Cathedral.

Tuesday, *1st June*.—A " 150 " strikes the truncated tower to the right of the south cross-bar, in the shaft of a counterfort under the pinnacle; the little grotesque statue in the angle is shattered. A "150" knocks down three small columns in the lower part of the open staircase of the north tower, biting deeply into the stone at the point of junction of the turret and the tower (Plate 71).

Tuesday, 15*th June.*—A "150" makes a very wide breach in the upper part of the same staircase of the north tower (Plate 71). Another decrowns the pinnacle of the third counterfort of the nave (south side); a fall of stone breaks the gargoyle of the neighbouring counterfort, on the left—a big dog's head. A third, on the same side, violently shakes the end of the high gallery close to the tower; the two first arcatures are overthrown, and the base knocked to pieces (Plate 72); still on the same side, the lower spring of the buttress of the fourth counterfort has been hit from underneath. The roofs of the low nave in this region are strewn with small débris of architecture thrown down by the explosions of these three shells. Finally, on the south tower, a shrapnel shell, and another on the great roofs at the crossing of the transept, under the north arch.

Sunday, 27*th June.*—A "150" falls in the rear courtyard, in the Rue du Cloître between the Cathedral and the chapel of the Archbishop's palace; a fragment breaks off, and throws over, at the lower gallery of the chevet, one of two small columns knocked down on the 22nd November, which had remained for seven months propped against the balustrade (Plate 65); another fragment strikes, at the third stage of the transept, the beautiful corner statue which personifies the Church in company with the Synagogue, and breaks the right arm and the left hand (Plate 83).

Pl. 77

Photo de l'*Illustration*

THE BURNED QUARTERS AROUND THE CATHEDRAL, IN 1918 (*see p. 150; face p. 140*)

Pl. 78

THE FAÇADE OF THE SOUTH TRANSEPT *(see pp. 168 and 171)*

Photos Antony Thouret

PIER AT THE ANGLE OF THE TRANSEPT *(see p. 168; face p. 141)*

The Disaster

Saturday, 3rd July.—A " 150 " on the roof under the arch of the transept at the beginning of the central vault.

Wednesday, 21st July.—A " 150 " shell strikes the shaft of the second counterfort of the apse (south side), breaks up the block of masonry, and shatters in its recoil the framework of the window from top to bottom (Plate 73). The three stained glass windows of this chapel were previously destroyed on the 8th of April ; this time the entire framework of iron and stone has been torn away and broken into fragments ; cross, candlesticks, reliquaries—everything on the altar has been swept away like wisps of straw ; the confessionals are overturned, and chairs have been projected far into the nave. Another breaks up the lower gallery of the chevet, above the Chapel of the Blessed Sacrament, at its point of juncture with the buttress, the fourth on the north side (Plate 74).

Tuesday, 19th October.—A " 150 " in the bottom parts of the buttress at the angle of the north tower.

1916. *Sunday, 2nd April.*[1]—A shell on the first buttress of the apse (south side) ; the explosions demolish the framework of the window in the Rosary chapel and riddle the covering of boards and sand protecting the retable of the altar. Another on the seventh buttress of the nave (south side) at the height of the second row of windows. An apsidal chapel is struck by the splinters of a third which fell on a neighbouring house in the Rue du Cloître.

Tuesday, 11th July.—(A bad night—one thousand five

---

[1] I left Reims on the 21st of January, 1916, but without losing sight of my poor Cathedral. Minute notes have kept me in touch with the catastrophes and the smallest incidents, so that I have been able, from a distance, to continue up to the last day this mournful enumeration of the bombardment of which it has been the victim.

hundred shells.) A shell crashes through the ceiling of the south transept, above the Fonts. This is the second time that the ceiling has been broken open ; the breach is much more serious than that of the 21st of February, 1915 ; it measures 1 m. 50 by 80 centimetres. But the double arch is not struck. Stones have been projected with such violence that a bar of the choir grill on the other side of the sanctuary has been cut clean. A second shell breaks up the pavement, at the angle of the Great Entrance, near the north tower.

Friday, 27th October.—(A thousand shells.) A shell at the base of the second buttress of the south tower seriously damages the masonry and blows into fragments some pieces of sculpture, single columns, chapters, fragments of gargoyles, and grimacing heads which had been left over from the old restoration, and were placed there, between the two buttresses. Another, of large calibre, crushes, over a surface of two square metres, at the level of the high windows, the archivolt of one of the great bays above the south transept (facing west). A shrapnel shell peppers the buttresses and windows of the apse, towards the centre, high up. Three other shells have fallen in the courts, and four in the immediate neighbourhood.

   .   .   .   .   .   .

It has been said, and the information is well founded, for I have seen the documents at Rome—that the Pope intervened with the German Emperor in May, 1915, to ask that Reims Cathedral might at length be spared ; that Cardinal von Hartmann of Cologne, having been charged with the message, had transmitted to the Holy Father after

Pl. 79

Photo Gemper

THE BROKEN CEILING ABOVE THE SANCTUARY (*see p.* 168; *face p.* 142)

Pl. 80

Photos Gemper

THE BROKEN VAULTINGS IN THE CHOIR AND THE NAVES *(see p. 168; face p. 143)*

an interview with the Kaiser, the Imperial answer, and that a couple of days later a letter from Chancellor Bethmann-Hollweg confirmed the Cardinal's report.

Regrets were expressed, and a promise was made ; it is contrary to his wish, and only under the constraint of necessity, that the wonderful Cathedral was bombarded, because the French were using it for military purposes ; that if they insisted upon acting thus, it would be necessary to recommence, but that for the future he promised this— neither the generals nor the corps commanders who are in command before Reims should be judges of the occasion of bombardments, for which Great General Headquarters alone should be responsible.

One must believe that Great General Headquarters has on several occasions given such orders, for in the months which followed, up to the terrible days of the spring of 1917, the Cathedral was bombarded at least nine times, and received twenty-two shells.

And why ? Since nothing has been changed, nothing has been moved, and, unless they have been subject to hallucinations they have not seen either a military post, or signals, or anything whatever there, where there is nothing to see.

.   .   .   .

This third winter has made serious ravages. The plaster, soaked by the rains, and rotted by the frost, has in several places fallen in enormous masses ; large cakes, detached from the high ceilings, have spun round in their fall, and smashed on the stones with the sinister and heavy noise of a distant explosion, the echo of which has disturbed the naves, and alarmed the surrounding quarters.

143

When it rains the water runs in streams in the Cathedral, for the showers and storms which fall on the roof pass through, and descend in cascades on the pavement, then slowly drain into streams and lie about, here, there, and everywhere, where the ground has yielded, in greenish patches which add to this picture of desolation a note of indescribable forlornness.

Meanwhile prayer has not altogether ceased in the profaned sanctuary. Every Friday the Cardinal of Reims comes here alone to make the Stations of the Cross, in this tragic atmosphere, amid this infinite sadness ; and this golden thread connects the past with the triumphal hour of restoration.

In the month of October, 1916, the Holy Father, to whom we owe so much of generous initiative throughout this terrible war, again intervened at Berlin, in order to obtain some respite for the Cathedral which would have permitted the undertaking of the most urgent works of cover and protection.

Of course, the Kaiser could not accede to this request of the Pope without demanding guarantees, which it would have been quite easy to give him, that the Cathedral was not in fact utilized for military purposes. But the reply, in addition to the fact that it was delayed until the end of December, pushed demands so far as to be equivalent to a refusal. For, if the first two conditions—no soldiers in the courtyards, and no batteries within a radius of eight hundred metres—were reasonable, the third exceeded all reason—immunity for eighteen named villages on the German front, with a vague clause that " any attack directed, *from the environs of Reims*, against their

144

lines " should release the Imperial Government from its promise.

The Cathedral nevertheless enjoyed a long respite during this winter of 1916–17, and even during the first half of April, when the town, in that feverish time which preceded the offensive, was scourged and bruised as in the worst days. They arranged it, undoubtedly. It was not a loyal and frank abstention. They varied ; from time to time they dealt it sly blows. But these shame-faced and isolated attacks were well separated, as if they did not dare to do more.

We hoped so. We thought we had at last touched bottom with our troubles, and that after the horrors of 1914 and 1915 we should see nothing worse ; it seemed to us that the instinct for evil did not know how to go further in the way of producing tears and suffering—when, suddenly, towards mid-April, they succeeded in surpassing themselves.

They brag of their genius for inflicting injury ; they congratulate themselves upon it. They did not wish it to be said that a single crime had gone uncommitted, that they had forgotten anything ; that a wickedness was still possible, and they had not had the idea of it ; that there was at their cannon's mouth some beautiful, great, sacred thing, and they had left it standing.

So without thinking more of the assurances given to the Pope than of a scrap of paper, without bothering their heads about the world's clamour, without emotion before the spectacle of this mutilated but yet living splendour— " only to see it is to become a Catholic "—the Crown Prince (it was he who commanded on this front) in cold blood gave the order to strike it again, and to strike it harder.

L   145

So, on the 16th of April, about three o'clock, after some overlong shots which lost themselves in the Rue Libergier, on the Parvis, and several others which wandered to right and left, some large calibre shells, such as one had not yet seen at Reims—" 240's, 305's, and 340's "—came full upon their objective—fourteen that day ; more than twenty on Thursday the 19th, and two on the 21st ; on the 24th, the worst day of that terrible week, in the uproar of explosions which shake the sky and make the earth tremble, no one is able to count the number.

Truly, as Heinrich Heine said, " it is their God Thor who hammers the Cathedral with his fury."

The smoke of the explosions mounts higher than the towers. At five points at least the ceilings are breached, one of the mistress piles of the transept is half broken ; both the towers are struck, the flying buttresses broken ; at the chevet, in that wonderful maze of stone, of arches, pinnacles, turrets, columns, angels, animals, statues of every kind, it is a veritable carnage.

In the face of such a cynical, savage relapse into crime Cardinal Luçon, for the second time, cried out his protest to the world : " Grievously affected by the new blows aimed at my Cathedral and at several churches of my episcopal city, under the pretext of military use, I declare that I know of a certainty, and I affirm, that neither the Cathedral nor any of the churches of Reims has been used for military purposes."

Benedict XV again intervened ; he wrote to the Kaiser. The Imperial Government replied, in July, that the French had made Reims the centre of their spring offensive and established " *un gran numero di batterie sotto la protezione*

Pl. 81

Photo Gemper

THE RAVAGED APSE (*see p.* 170; *face p.* 146)

Pl. 82

Photos Gemper

DETAILS OF THE APSE (see Pl. 62) (see p. 170; face p. 147)

della Cathedrale," and so had made it impossible to spare the monument. It added that it ill became the French to make a grievance of the matter when their own army systematically bombarded the Basilica of St. Quentin. This was a triple falsehood.

The Archbishop of Reims is not responsible for what happened on the Aisne front, at St. Quentin ;[1] but, sticking always to his post, at the very foot of the Cathedral, in his own house, from which twenty shells had not been able to expel him, he knew what passed under his own eyes, at his own door, and is qualified to tell us.

In his reply of the 30th of July to the Holy Father he establishes : (1) That Reims was not the centre of the

[1] It was at the beginning of July that the German newspapers began to accuse the French of bombarding the basilica of St. Quentin. On the 9th of July the French command denied this, declaring that " formal orders have been given to the artillery not to fire on the town, and above all not upon the Cathedral." The Archpriest of St. Quentin, from whom I sought precise information, wrote me on the 7th October, 1917, that " the town was evacuated on the 18th of March, 1917, but that on several occasions before that date the Germans had used the steeple as an observation post, and that some months before the evacuation, they installed wireless telegraphy in the belfry. *Notwithstanding that, never, from the 28th April, 1914, to the 18th March, 1917, did the French artillery fire a single shell upon the basilica.*

" On the 1st of July, 1916, an English airman dropped some bombs on the station, which struck some dynamite wagons. A formidable explosion devastated the entire quarter, and the concussion was so violent that nine or ten large windows in the basilica, 1600 metres from the station, were broken.

" *At once the German press announced that the French had shelled, and almos destroyed, the Cathedral.*

" Well before the 15th of August, the day of the fire, in the northern sector, five kilometres from the town, French troops had replaced the British, who, tired of seeing observers on the edifices, threatened to fire on the town." (*Demaret, Archpriest of St. Quentin.*)

The German *communiqué* of the 16th of August, which accuses the French of having fired 1600 incendiary shells upon the town on the 15th, has thus, to say the least, an appearance of improbability.

To whom do they impute the mine holes drilled in the big pillars of the nave, which were found after their departure, and reproduced in photographs ? (See *Illustration*, October, 1918.)

battle, since the April offensive was launched, not in the Reims front, but at Moronvillers, twenty kilometres to the east, and Brimont, ten kilometres to the north ; (2) that at no single moment was there, around the Cathedral or in its vicinity, a single battery of artillery, and that, consequently, nothing was easier than to direct fire upon the batteries where they actually were, without any risk of hitting the Cathedral ; and (3) that the bombardments of the 16th, 19th, 21st, 22nd, and 24th April were delivered directly and persistently upon the Cathedral, without seeking for mythical batteries around the Cathedral at all. And he ends by saying : " This note is not only the conscientious expression of a sincere conviction ; it is the statement of an eye-witness who relates what he has seen."

After this outburst in April came a repetition of the treacherous work of the preceding months. " They did not intend it," but the shells came on their own account ! One on the 14th of June, three on the 28th, two on the 29th, and one on the 26th of July. During the night of the 25th–26th, about three o'clock in the morning, under the shock of an explosion or of a fall of stone, the great bell struck—a lugubrious note which had not been heard for three years, sounding like a groan in the silence of the night. There was another shell on the 30th of July, three on the 13th August, two on the 23rd, one on the 28th, one on the 18th of December, one on the 16th of February, 1918, one on the 18th of March, and four on the 21st. At that point my information stops.

One might think that these figures corresponded to a period of lull ; there were, on the contrary, during that winter, some stormy days, and if the Cathedral was not

Pl. 83

Photos Antony Thouret

THE STATUE OF THE NEW LAW, COMPLETELY DESTROYED IN 1918 (*see p. 171*)

THE STATUE OF OUR LORD AT THE ENTRANCE OF THE NORTH TRANSEPT
(*see p. 140; face p. 148*)

Pl. 84

Photo Sainsaulieu

THE HIGH GALLERY, AT THE CROSSING OF THE SOUTH TRANSEPT *(see p. 171; face p. 149)*

struck then, it is plain proof that they only hit it when they intended to do so.

I am not writing the history of Reims ; others will do that. But, sombre as was the horizon during those long months of the 1914–1915 winter, the most sombre spirits, those which were most impervious to hope, would have exclaimed their incredulity if any one had suggested the idea that two, three, four years later nothing would be changed, that the German batteries would still encircle the town from Brimont to Nogent, and that on the 28th of March, 1918, the last determined inhabitants withstanding this cruel siege, some hundreds of them, would be forcibly evacuated with the Cardinal and the Mayor, at a few hours' notice, after having seen break, upon their ruins and their own heads, tempests such as they had not known in the worst days. It was better not to know it ; they could not have endured to the end, if they had known.

At the most critical hour, when, in their savage rush, the Germans suddenly found themselves once more on the Marne, menacing Paris, a breath from on high, as in September, 1914, in a moment changed the aspect. Victory made a pact with our armies, and, in the course of that gigantic battle, in which Foch, that intrepid soldier, that great Christian of ours, saved the fortunes of France and the civilization of the world, it came about that on the 5th of October, 1918, the city was at last freed.

I say " the city," because, when they have a soul, cities do not die, and if it is no more than a heap of cinders and ruins it keeps within its soul those virile energies which are the earnest of resurrection.

They continued, from March to October, by slow stages,

their work of destruction, while the battle raged ; they pushed that work, by steel and fire, to the utmost limit ; with furious bombardments—of twenty thousand, thirty thousand shells, with methodical burning of everything they had not already burned, sixty hectares at the least devoured by the flames. And that zone of desolation around the Cathedral now accentuates the air of tragic and forsaken melancholy. (Plate 77).

It has itself endured terrible assaults, whose phases no one has noted ;[1] but, in this orgy of coldly calculated malice beneath which Reims sank, beaten and beaten again like iron hammered on the anvil, the Cathedral has not been submerged, because Providence wished to leave us this consolation in our distress.

[1] I have since been enabled to consult on the spot the official notes of Commandant Lexa, Major of the Place, made from the daily reports of the gendarmerie post which watched the Cathedral, during the four months of evacuation. And I have gathered from them the following figures : the 25th June, 4 shells ; the 26th July, 3 ; the 29th, 15 ; the 31st, 5 ; in August, on the 7th, 3 ; on the 8th, 10 ; on the 12th, 15 ; on the 14th, 6 ; on the 17th, 2 ; on the 20th, 23 ; on the 25th, 10 ; on the 7th September, 15 ; on the 17th, 17.

We thus get a total of 287 shells, 42 of which were before the fire, and 245 in the four years following it. See Appendix C. List of shells which struck the Cathedral.

VI

THE FUTURE

CHAPTER VI

THE FUTURE

[This chapter, written in 1915, no longer reflects the exact situation. But for two and a half years it corresponded with the facts. It described a condition of things and a condition of mind. It presented the position as it was after the first outrage; but there have been two, or rather three, of these outrages, and they must not be confused. It marks the stages, and corresponds to the successive phases of the disaster.

In this way it retains a documentary value, and has its raison d'être : *it is a landmark of which we have need in order that we may take the measure of other crimes which were still more disastrous for the Cathedral than was the first; for the worst wounds, those which were inflicted in its vital parts, do not date from September, 1914, but from the spring of 1917 and the evil days of 1918.]*

O N the 6th of May, 1210, the Carlovingian Cathedral of Ebbon and Hincmar collapsed in a fearful conflagration which, like that of September, 1914, devoured a part of the city. The existing Cathedral was born of that catastrophe.

Religious architecture had just entered upon a new phase; the robust Roman arcade was made lighter, and rose into a pointed arch.

Already, at St. Denis, at Noyon, at Sens, at Senlis, and above all, at Laon, near Paris, there had been built superb churches in which this upward movement was displayed in greater boldness, in more suppleness, and with greater

153

dignity at each stage. And, under the inspiration of a master mason, whose name is forgotten, but who was a genius, the mediæval style had found, in the restoration of the Church at Chartres, after the fire of 1194, its definite orientation.

At the dawn of this Thirteenth century, which awaited St. Louis, and marked the apogee of the Christian social order, cathedrals sprang up in a splendid efflorescence of stone—a sublime effort of Art and Faith stretching towards Heaven.

The Archbishop of Reims, Albéric de Humbert, did not hesitate long. It was his design to rebuild his church upon a vaster plan, with the ambition of surpassing anything hitherto accomplished. And, on the anniversary of the disaster, on the 6th of May, 1211, he laid the first stone of our Cathedral.

Thirty years later the choir was built ; and the Chapter said its Office there.

Before the end of the century the whole church was opened to worship.[1] It took nearly two centuries more, of troublous times, before the upper parts of the edifice were built and adorned.

In 1481 there remained to erect only the steeples on the towers at the Entrance ; the architects had realized Jean d'Orbais' conception of genius, the magnificent synthesis of power, of grace, and of beauty. Our Lady of Reims— the church of kings and the queen of churches[2]—appeared, in her virginal charm, like an evocation of religious majesty

---

[1] In the Thirteenth century Reims built, not only its cathedral, but that other marvel of Gothic art, the choir of St. Rémi and St. Nicaise.

[2] *The Cathedral of Reims*, by C. Eulart. See *L'Art et les Artistes*, special number.

154

descended upon earth ; when suddenly a common accident, a fire started inadvertently in the roof, put this marvel into the same lamentable state into which the Germans have again plunged it to-day.

It was the 24th of July, 1481. As yesterday, everything which could burn did burn. The vaultings were stripped ; the lead, the timber, the great central bell-tower, the steeple of the chevet, the flies of the transept, were destroyed, and the bells broken and melted. On the morrow, the 25th of July, in capitular assembly, restoration was decided, and in the week which followed they set about the preparation of estimates and the discussion of ways and means.

In 1515 Our Lady had recovered her beauty.

The Revolution confiscated and profaned, but without doing very much damage ; so that since the Fifteenth century the Cathedral has suffered only from the ravages of time. But the slow and hidden eating away of time is enough to make ruins ; stones have their old age and their decrepitude. The partial restorations in the first half of the Nineteenth century were only palliatives.

In 1875 the Archbishop of Reims, Mgr. Langénieux, rightly preoccupied with the state of dilapidation which each winter grew worse, drew the attention of the Government to the urgency of an immediate and complete restoration. On the 23rd of October he received at his table four Ministers, who were his friends—M. Dufaure, Minister of Justice, M. Wallon, Minister of Public Instruction and Worship, M. Léon Say, Minister of Finance, and M. Caillaux, Minister of Public Works, with the Prefects of the Marne and the Ardennes, the Mayor of Reims, and others.

Conducted by the architect, M. Millet, he made with

them a minute inspection of the building from the foundations to the summit. He showed them the disquieting cracks, the holes, the shaking stones, the statues eaten away and worn by rain, the broken gutters, through which water filtered into the walls, the denuded counterforts, the crevice in the Entrance, the subsidence of the Great Rose. And, up above, in the galleries, he held a little Cabinet council while they were still actually under the lively impression made by their inspection ; there was no shadow of fundamental disagreement among them ; in desire they were in concord ; there were some exchanges of views as to the methods of procedure ; and their regard was then turned upon the Minister of Finance. M. Léon Say drew from his pocket a sealed envelope. " This," he said, " is the state of the Budget ; it has been sent to me this morning, and I have not yet opened it." It declared a surplus of seventy-six million francs ; the cause of Our Lady was won.

On the 21st of December Parliament voted, with the necessary credits, by annuities, the complete restoration of the Cathedral of Reims.[1]

For forty years, without intermission, with respect, with

---

[1] On the 26th of June, 1876, the Archbishop blessed the yards where the work was to be commenced, and the architects deposited, at the right angle of the niche of the seventh counterfort (middle façade) under the dripstone, this inscription of an epigraphy without elegance, but which witnesses the part in the restoration which belongs to Cardinal Langénieux :—

French Republic
Under the Presidency of Marshal MacMahon
at the instance of
Monseigneur Langénieux
Archbishop of Reims
On the 21st December 1875
A Law was passed
For the Restoration of the Cathedral.

Pl. 85

LATERAL COUNTERFORTS (SOUTH SIDE)

Photos Gemper

LATERAL COUNTERFORTS (NORTH SIDE) (see p. 172; face p. 156)

Pl. 86

Photo Thinot.

THE TOWERS, SEEN FROM BEHIND, IN 1914

Photo Gemper

THE TOWERS, SEEN FROM BEHIND, IN 1918 (*see p.* 172; *face p.* 157)

love, the architects employed themselves. They took the work stone by stone. At the moment of the declaration of war this labour, the most considerable, the most conscientious which has been accomplished since the Fifteenth century, had almost reached its end ; a few months more, and it would be finished. Our Lady of Reims, freed at length from the last of her scaffoldings, would be restored to us in her rejuvenated splendour, ready to defy the ages !

Like a savage beast the German passed ; he defiled, he mutilated, he ravaged. He reduced all this effort to nothing !

1210 ! 1481 ! 1914 ! Dolorous and tragic dates, which call to, and answer, each other in the sinister gleam of conflagrations !

Our ancestors of the Thirteenth and the Fifteenth centuries, powerless as we are in the face of the like disaster, must have felt that same sense of prostration which we have experienced.

Did they recall, as they gazed upon their ruins, the vision of Ezechiel, and the words, " Can these dry bones live ? " In any case they recovered themselves. Twice the inspiration which vivifies accomplished the miracle ; it reanimated their courage ; it raised the stones again ; the Cathedral was resuscitated.

The past compels us. That tenacity of our fathers which never permitted them to confess themselves beaten, but urged them to begin again without a pause, traces for us our duty to-day.

If the Cathedral, as was said, as was believed for a moment, had been destroyed, it is likely that, whatever one

157

might have wished, France, exhausted by the war, would have felt herself incapable of rebuilding it ; we are no longer in the Thirteenth century. But since it is not thrown down, since the bulk of the work has not been affected, since essential parts have resisted, since the arches have not fallen in, since it is reparable; to repair it is for us, in the face of the world, simply a question of dignity and pride.

She must be healed, this great wounded thing—wounded in the war. She wants to rise again with France. And we will raise her.

Those who say No—there are some—love it as much as we do. Their hearts have trembled like ours. Only, in a first access of anger, they have been more concerned with avenging the victim than with healing its wounds. But this Yes and this No are brothers ; they proceed from the same feeling ; they rejoin in a common homage to Our Lady of Reims.

Poets have cried out their indignation in vibrant pages which are—songs of poets, and which have stirred our emotions.

> " I would that they kept her without repair,
> The church as she stands now, stricken and bare,
> Her gaping wounds to the world arrayed,
> Let no effort to close them be ever essayed "[1]—

that we may " inflame hatred and prevent forgetfulness and render amnesty impossible for ever."

To follow out this reasoning we should need to apply

[1] Miguel Zamaçoïs :—

> Je voudrais qu'on gardât sans y toucher du tout
> Le monument blessé tant qu'il tiendra debout.
> Avec ses trous béants, avec ses meurtrissures,
> Sans s'aviser jamais de panser ses blessures.

Pl. 87

Photo Gemper

RAVAGES ON THE NORTH TOWER, AND GENERAL VIEW (*see p. 172; face p. 158*)

Pl. 88

Photo Sainsaulieu

A VIEW ACROSS THE RUINS *(face p. 159)*

it to all our ravaged towns, treat them like dead cities, like Pompeii, in order that " revenge may the better preserve its vigour, and that the more easily hatred may come back to the heart through the eyes."

And I see, in a study in which their arguments are summed up, that they have not only thought, but they have said, they have dared to write this : " We adjure Arras, Malines, Louvain, all the towns of ravaged Belgium, to guard their injuries intact, and to show them without cessation to the passers-by of posterity."[1]

This adjuration, it appears, has attained such consistency that the Belgian Government has thought it incumbent to answer it. Thus : " Belgium has no need to conserve, as some have proposed, her ruined buildings, in order to re-mind herself of her misfortunes. She has the ambition to regain her former integrity. A monument in each district bearing the names of soldiers who have died for their country and of murdered inhabitants, and a commemorative inscription on every edifice rebuilt, will suffice to recall the past to us."[2]

The poets again, in order to brand the vandals, have said, calling up a vision of the sublime ruins of Greek temples on the Acropolis :

" A shame for them ; for us a Parthenon ! "[3]

But can one assimilate Our Lady of Reims to the Parthenon ?

[1] See *Illustration* of 3rd March, 1915.

[2] Report of the Minister of Public Works on the reconstruction of buildings and destroyed villages. See *Moniteur Belge,* October, 1915.

[3] Ed. Rostand.

The Cathedral of Reims

When the guns ravaged the Parthenon it was already dead. It was an empty temple, a temple deserted by a cult long extinct, a body without a soul, a superb body which no longer had its pagan soul to reanimate it. When the catastrophe fell it added to beauty the majesty of great ruins ; it has been kept thus that it might be the better admired.

Our Lady of Reims was struck in the full flow of life, in the full vigour of her activity. She has her reason for existence always ; she has not finished her mission. She has been wounded, she is bruised, like France and with France, in the same combats ; but she has not given way, she has not fallen, any more than France has. She stands erect. She does not want to die ! And how can she die, unless France dies ? Without this sanctuary, this diadem, without her Cathedral

" The France of to-morrow will be no more the same."[1]

Have they not talked also of transforming her into a museum, where she may display the débris of her glory, and become the cemetery of her own grandeur ; or, again, an ossuary in which may be reassembled the remains of our unknown soldiers now dispersed in our fields by the chances of war ? It is a pious and patriotic thought, which will be realized some day, but elsewhere and otherwise.

We cannot turn into a necropolis the Cathedral of Reims, the baptistery and cradle of Christian France, any more than we can leave her in her sublime distress, in order to hand her over to-morrow, like the rest of the notable ruins, to the careless and frivolous curiosity of tourists. That

[1] P. Dubois.

indeed would be sacrilege. To-day we say : " Sacred relic
of a profaned temple, trophy of a crime, which cries for
vengeance, and which the pilgrims of patriotism, of art,
and of faith approach with respect ! " Those are sincere
words, but they have no endurance ; for them there is no
to-morrow.

I imagine that if the old architects of the Middle Ages
who in ecstasy[1] conceived this poem in stone, who stone
by stone created and built and chiselled this work of splendour—Jean d'Orbais, Jean le Loup, Gaucher de Reims,
Bernard de Soissons, Robert de Coucy, and the others—
were called to deliberate in 1919 upon the fate of the Cathedral, they would have eyes only for it ; the idea of con-
founding the German by leaving it a battered ruin would
never enter their heads. They would not resign themselves to a defeat. They would think to avenge it more
surely by compensating for the outrage with an increase of
glory : " You defiled her because she was beautiful ; we
will make her more beautiful." They would betake themselves to the task with passion, with all their soul ; they
would take up again the work which the past centuries have
achieved ; they would make her rise, with her spires, in
triumph to the skies.

Is that a dream ?

If to-morrow one attempted it, would the towers support the spires ? We fear they would not.

But at any rate let us go as far on the road as possible ;
for France—France as she is to-day, without distinction of
opinions and creeds—has declared so loudly how much store

---

[1] " The artists who made that," writes Rodin, speaking of Our Lady of Reims,
" threw into the world a reflection of the divinity."

M

she sets by it that she cannot refuse to restore to herself *her own Cathedral.*

At the Beaux Arts, at the Historical Monuments Commission, they are all well disposed to the work. They wish to save all that can be saved, and repair everything that is reparable.

Besides, why should we to-day treat Our Lady of Reims otherwise than we have always up to now treated the Cathedrals of France ?

They are part of the national patrimony. They have been built to last for all time. They survive the centuries which witnessed their birth and trusted to the others to see that they should not die. Each generation, solid with the past, responsible for the future, has given them a helping hand, has brought to them its stone with a solicitude constantly increasing, for the more they age the more are they loaded with memories, the more venerable they become, the more we love and admire them.

Have we not repaired, and to the best of our ability (among many others), Our Lady of Paris, St. Denis, St. Front de Perigneux, the façade of Rouen, Laon, Soissons, the Wonder of Mont St. Michel . . . and Our Lady of Reims ?

At Reims they have but to resume and continue the work already in train for nearly half a century past. It appears even that the Law of December, 1875, which is not abrogated, suffices to cover the principle at least of that restoration.

The question of expense, heavy though it might be, would not be an obstacle. France victorious will find again the days of prosperity.

Pl. 89

PANORAMIC VIEW *(face p. 162)*

Pl. 90

Photo Thinot

PANORAMIC VIEWS (face p. 163)

The Future

The attack upon Our Lady of Reims has not been swamped in the mass of depredations which this army of savages has left behind it. It stands out ; it has a meaning which the others have not. It is, as it has been called, " the German Crime," the direct insult to France, the reparation of which should have been a separate article in the treaty of peace. Such a recognition and punishment would have made an impression upon their pride more than could the mute lesson of ruins, too delicate for them to comprehend, and with which they cynically feed their vanity : " We have beaten it down ; they have not known how to build it up. The last word rests with our guns."

And, to emphasize the import of what they have done, and spread the shame of it in the full light of day, so that neither we nor the others should be tempted to forget, instead of inflicting upon ourselves the harrowing spectacle of those despoiled masterpieces, let us engrave upon each side of the Entrance, in the manner of Tacitus—the place is quite ready[1]—two avenging inscriptions, which shall publish upon the restored work a double record of their impotence and their villainy ; and in front, on the Parvis, with raised muzzles and gaping mouths, like chained beasts, two of the huge German guns which spat out their venom on Our Lady of Reims.

And, that it may speak to the eyes, we will have a perpetual exposition in the Treasure of the Cathedral, in our war museum, of the sacred relics of the martyrdom, the precious ruins of statues, the fragments of sculpture, remnants of stained glass, small pieces of art, atoms of beauty,

[1] The smooth surface of the two end buttresses, right and left of the entrance, 4 m. 15 high by 3 m. 55 wide.

with the shell-splinters which mutilated them ; bits of our melted bells, trickles of lead fixed in the mouth of gargoyles, twisted ironwork of past ages—like so many pieces of evidence, so that the most wearied mind and the most humble soul may remember, and be indignant.

Everyone agrees that we must preserve a palpable and irrefutable proof of the crime. But we should be able to do this while shaming Germany, without at the same time humiliating the Cathedral. And I am more at ease therefore in approaching a delicate question which is still being discussed among architects and artists the most resolved upon prompt reparation—the statues of the Entrance.

There are many who upon this point make reservations. That we should restore the edifice, they say, that we should give it back its old appearance, its character, its architectural lines, that we should restore its atmosphere of prayer, its silence, its soul, its liturgical life, its singing, the royal splendour of its religious solemnities—yes ; but to touch the statues of the Entrance would be a sacrilege.

It is a dual feeling which makes them talk in this way— the ever-present desire to perpetuate the odious memory, and the apprehension that the beauty of the work will be spoiled if hands are laid upon it.

This desire to furnish a pillory is legitimate ; but since we can do that in another manner, we ought not to sacrifice the splendour of the Cathedral to that object.

To what extent is fear of unskilful reparation really justified ? Evidently in this connection the word " irreparable," in the wide sense of the term, is applicable. The Thirteenth century, the century of great faith and of great

164

Pl. 91

Photo Thinot

PANORAMIC VIEWS (*face p. 164*)

Pl. 92

Photo Thinot

VIEW OF THE CATHEDRAL ACROSS THE RUINS FROM BURNT QUARTERS *(face p. 165)*

art, had put its mark upon those wonderful stones—" the noblest in all the world," said Montalembert—and time softly, with caresses, had added that warmth of colour which gave them the softened tone of old Florentine bronzes. We cannot recover that. But is that to say that we can recover nothing ? To put oneself into this too special point of view, is to risk losing the true point of view.

If we take these marvellous statues (of which the poorest is a masterwork) one by one, and consider them separately, isolated, each according to its own intrinsic value, as one does some rare piece in a museum, then, the original lost, all is lost. One does not restore a statue of the Thirteenth century, any more than one does an antique marble.

But we are looking at the Cathedral. It is necessary to step back a pace. These missing statues were part of the building. They were simply a detail of its ornamentation, superb flowers of an immense sheaf. And it is with reference to the Entrance, with a view to the effect of the ensemble, and not only in regard to their individual charm, that we must appreciate them. And then we have not the right to be so restricted in our judgment. Has the Entrance of Our Lady of Reims the need of this element for its completeness, for the full recovery of its beauty, its integrity, its grand air of triumphal majesty ?—Yes or no ?

There is no question of reconstitution by guesswork. The documents which will ensure rigorous precision are not lacking, and to avow impotence in the matter is to insult French art of the Twentieth century. Our great artists, the masters of French sculpture, ought, in a fine spirit of patriotic faith, to apportion among themselves the task, and each one of them should claim the honour of making one of these masterpieces live again, as an act of homage to Our Lady of Reims.

One wonders how many among those who hesitate have been too much impressed by regrettable exaggerations in the Press. The pen trembles when one insists a little upon this argument. One fears to furnish a pretext to exaggeration the other way, and to appear to attenuate the crime of the Germans. We wish neither to attenuate nor to magnify ; and when one discovers and points out with relief that the victim has been able to support such blows without dying, one is not in the least degree condoning the assassin's act.

Let us then take the Cathedral in the state in which they left it ; the damage is grave enough to render it superfluous to add anything.

Half of the great Entrance has been destroyed ; that is incontestable. With tears in our eyes, and death in our soul, we have counted the injuries ; and our poor written words are too cold to make those who have not seen it really understand how inexpressibly distressing they are. A painter, with his colours, would have more success.

But among these ravaged masses of sculpture, it is nevertheless true to say that, of the thirty-five great statues in the porches, to which may be added the thirteen of the north entrance, only five have lost their heads : the Queen of Saba, the angel of St. Nicaise, the young deacon (opposite), a St. Rémi, and his neighbour. When it is remembered that we have been able to recover the heads of the Queen of Saba and the angel, that castings of this angel and the Queen of Saba are in the museum of Comparative Sculpture at the Trocadéro, and that the others have been photographed a score of times, it must be admitted that the word " irreparable " is reduced to less tragic proportions.

They are all there, then, save five, whose absence mars the ensemble—these wonderful figures of virgins, of angels, and of saints who are no longer on earth, but who live, as in a trance, with features and expression of countenance so obviously belonging to our race ; with that smiling grace, which reflects goodness through their beauty, and seems to bring Heaven down to us. It will be easy to remake these five without recourse to the replicas at Bamberg, even if it be admitted, as some contend without proof yet, that the Master of Bamberg is our " Gaucher de Reims," precisely he who worked our arches and Entrances.

Of the seventy-five groups which decorate the arching of the façade I reckon that half a dozen are totally destroyed and ten seriously injured, but the heads of six of these have not been touched.

Finally, on the devastated reverse of the side porches of the Entrance, out of thirty-two statuettes, seventeen heads remain in their place, or have been recovered.

In these conditions the task, reduced to its proper proportions, does not appear to be more than it behoves us to undertake ; it is neither too arduous nor too complicated.

.   .   .   .

At this point we must take stock of some new disasters.

I wished to judge of them on the spot. I had revisited Reims, in 1916 and 1917, in the depths of its tribulation, and in melancholy solitude—an immense desert of cinder and ruins. I have since explored the Cathedral minutely, as a surgeon does a wounded man ; and, without staying upon a detailed description of new mutilations, I wish to note the most serious of them, and indicate their importance.

Up to the 16th of April, 1917, we said : she is decrowned, disfigured, riddled with wounds, grievously hurt in all her members, but the skeleton frame is not injured. We cannot say that to-day.

In the course of four days, in some hours, the " 305's " and the " 340's " did more harm than did the fire of 1914 and the three years of bombardment had accomplished ; the assaults of 1918 plunged it into a yet further degree of distress.

The worst blow was that which shook the corner pier at the south-east crossing of the transept (24th April, 1917).

M. Sansanlieu, the architect, who continued his efforts from day to day, more than once risking his life, was, it is true, able to foresee and provide against the danger ; but all this part of the Cathedral is in a pitiable condition (Plate 78).

The vaulting here and there is broken. I counted eight or nine openings lamentably cut out against the sky ; but to appreciate their proportions, one must go below and look at the accumulation of stones which are piled up like a mountain on the ground.

The most considerable is above the sanctuary (21st April, 1917) (Plate 79) ; a fall and some new blows in 1918 have finished by letting in the daylight over one gallery and half of the other. The high altar is buried beneath a heap of rubbish of eighty to one hundred cubic metres (Plate 80).

Above the lantern the break-through of the 21st February, 1915, the first and only one for nearly two years, not wider than a double hand's-breadth (Plate 67), was, in 1917, of the size of the *oculi* of the nave ; it was three times that in 1918.

In the transept, near the sacristies, the break-through of the 11th July, 1916, has also enormously increased.

On the pulpit side, the vaulting of the fifth bay has lost, besides its nerves, two of its counterforts, north and south ; it is open to the sky through a circular hole, just in the axis of the nave, reminding one of the great lucernaires of the catacombs.

Some paces away, at the foot of a pillar, lies intact a " 305," which made its entry at the seventh bay of the lower nave, without exploding. Farther away, two more bays, the ninth and tenth, are pierced ; pierced also is the vaulting of St. Joseph's chapel, in the apse. The other holes, above the throne in the choir behind, in the naves, at the bottom of the lower sacristy, and under the Hall of the Kings, are of less importance (1917).

In the great nave the ground is torn up by five shell holes.

What remains of the stained glass has fallen in the debacle. In 1918 I counted four windows totally destroyed and fourteen severely damaged ; now it is the framework which has gone, now the Rose.

Outside, it is above all the apse which produces an impression of devastation.

What wonderful eurythmy of lines enchants the eye in gazing at that zone of counterforts of the chevet ! What gracious effects of perspective ! What lightness in those double leaps of the flying buttresses which spring upwards from one pile to the other with the suppleness of the lianas of the forest! What a feeling of order and harmony and elegance, and at the same time of tranquil force and simplicity! It is indeed an enchantment to the eyes; one would say now that some monster had wallowed in fury amidst this beauty, like a wild boar in a flower-bed (Plates 81 and 82).

From the parting of the axis as far as the south transept the lattice-work balustrade which runs from one counterfort to the other is broken down; of the twelve fantastic animals which decorated it there remain but two, on the part which has escaped, the bull and the unicorn; farther away, the solitary elephant is decapitated (Plate 82); entire crowns of counterforts, niches, statues, pinnacles, have disappeared; four flights of flying buttresses are broken. On the roofs of the radiating chapels, great heads of gargoyles, débris of angels, of chimæras, monkeys, caryatides, still smiling or grimacing, pitched down pell-mell among the fallen stones, produce the effect of some horrible game of massacre.

I noticed in this region other injuries dating from 1918; important masses of masonry between the windows of the chapel of St. Cilinie have fallen; the high gallery has been struck at the junction of the second and third counterforts; the south face of the first counterfort of the transept is ravaged; only the statue remains intact on its broken pedestal, without niche, without pinnacle.

The havoc is continued along the façade of the south transept, and is much accentuated on the right; the shell of the 24th of April, 1917, which so badly injured the great pile at the corner of the choir, passed here, with many others. The turret of the staircase has been ripped open twice, and, of the four large niches which flank the Rose, not one has escaped, while the first, to the right, no longer exists (16th April, 1917) (Plate 78).

There is here an artistic loss to deplore ; the elegant statue of the New Law, which matches that of the Synagogue, and is connected, by motive and execution, with the Queen of Saba at the Great Entrance, has been destroyed. It had already been mutilated in 1917 (Plate 83).

Immediately after, over the length of several bays, the high gallery is pulverized ; the masonry has been pounded as in a mortar. Behind, on the roof, the great massive arches of the crossing of the transept bear traces of furious blows as of a battering-ram (Plate 84).

Along the nave four of the counterforts had already suffered, the fourth in particular, broken at the lower flight (1917) ; three others show deep injuries (1918) ; the sixth is decrowned ; the fifth has been shaken, and has lost its angel ; the whole of the first, that of the tower, has had half its cap cut away, exposing grave injuries below the drip-stone (Plate 85).

The bourdon-tower, hardly scratched up to then, has now also been as badly treated as the north tower ; at the height of the roof of the low nave, the great bay behind is staved in ; in the dark part of the staircase the axal column is thrown down and a complete block of four or five stairs has given way ; finally, of the open staircase there remains scarcely anything, the cage is empty up to the top, and a quarter of the cap of the tower is broken (1917).

The open staircase of the north tower, sad companion in misery, presents the same aspect of dilapidation, to such an extent that, since the 16th of April, 1917, had one wished, *it would have been impossible to ascend to the top of the towers, above all the south tower (Plate 86).*

In 1918, I noted in this north part the great damage which evidently corresponds with the famous observations in the Hindenburg Note. It is strange, nevertheless, that he should have mentioned the south tower four or five times, since it was the north tower only which had been struck.

The entire turret on the right is out of gear, from the base up to the beginning of the spire; its three small columns, so fine and so strong, are in bits; only the three capitals hang from the ironwork, unsupported. The little dome (which measures all the same six or seven metres) is in the air, without supports, like a dais above a statue; it is only held at one point, by adherence to the central tower (Plate 87).

The two turrets on the left, on the street side, have also had one of their columns broken.

Lower down, the big return counterforts have suffered much in their figured parts; those in the rear are smashed as far as the beginning of the Gallery of the Kings.

At the first counterfort of the nave, niche and turret have fallen to pieces; there remains the débris of an angel on the débris of a pedestal; the next has been roughly knocked about; the third is cut in two, and its upper flying buttress has been broken (16th April, 1917). The Gallery shows badly notched places (Plate 85).

At the right porch of the façade, in a part hitherto preserved, two of the large statues have been struck severely; the heads have fallen.

The Entrance at the north transept has suffered, and its

Pl. 93

Photos J. Puget

Photo Poirier

ACROSS THE RUINS (*face p. 172*)

Pl. 94

FROM THE AIR—1918 *(face p. 173)*

worst mutilations puzzled me on a first view ; the statue of our Lord, for instance, beneath its covering of sand-bags, is decapitated, without it appearing at first where the projectile hit it ; but the palisade has been renewed ; and, at the pediment of the door, the complete scene of St. Rémi chasing the incendiary devils, which Yencesse has so finely reproduced on the reverse of his medal " the Smile of Reims," has been carried away so neatly that one asks one-self how it was possible for a shell to do it without doing more damage to the groundwork.

One can note several explosions in the covings. Right up above, the turret of the counterfort on the left has been broken up, and the wirework of the Rose has been damaged.

The little protective wall which had been built there recently to guard the graceful figure of Eve has been broken down ; without this fragile shield, this delicate piece, which is evidently, if not from the same hand, yet from the same studio as the Virgin of the pier, would have been lost.

.   .   .   .   .   .

The above recitation is assuredly a serious one. It is incontestable that the situation has got worse. But in what way and to what degree ought this added misfortune to affect our resolutions ? In two points of view solely : time and money.

It will be longer, it will be more costly—much longer and much more costly ; but that is not of the essence of the matter.

Since the Cathedral still stands, and since its worst wounds are not mortal, the task, though rendered more delicate and

173

more laborious, remains a possible one, and our arguments retain their value.

There is still one argument which dominates all the others—the Faith. There should be no need to insist upon the weight we should give to that.

Patriotism, art, history, demand the restoration of Our Lady of Reims. Is it too much to say that Religion also demands it ?

Why did our fathers make it so beautiful, if not because they realized that they were building a temple to the Lord —a church—" the House of God " ? They knew that these words express something other than a mere religious affectation, in the sense in which other religious denominations use them ; they saw the eucharistic realities—the Altar, the Tabernacle ; they knew that our Catholic sanctuaries are, in the full meaning of the term, dwelling-places in which the Sacrament denotes the presence of God.

They worked for Our Lady, devotion to whom perfumed the Middle Ages throughout. It was the time when one said : *Regnum Galliae, Regnum Mariae !* For Christ men of arms went to battle in the Crusades. For Mary bishops and peoples built Cathedrals. For her nothing was too great, nothing too beautiful. And the genius of artists, stimulated by their faith, gave birth to this Marvel.

Now, since the Germans have committed this unforgettable crime of ravaging the Temple, of putting an end to worship and expelling Our Lady with their cannon, do not the same faith, the same piety, impose upon us the obligation to efface all traces of the sacrilege, to restore the Church, by lifting up the altar again, and giving back to the palace its splendour, so that the Queen may enter once more ?

Pl. 95

SPECIMENS OF "FAKED" PICTURE-POSTCARDS CIRCULATED IN 1915. THE STATUES
IN THE UPPER PHOTOGRAPH, PURPORTING TO BE FROM THE CENTRAL PORCH,
ARE ABSOLUTELY INTACT. THOSE IN THE LOWER PHOTOGRAPH, PURPORTING
TO REPRESENT THE CONDITION OF THE LEFT PORCH AFTER THE FIRE,
ARE QUITE WRONG. See Plates 23, 25, 26 (face p. 174)

Pl. 96

THE GREAT STATUES OF THE PORCHES UNDER SAND-BAGS *(face p. 175)*

The Future

In conclusion, it has been well said that " every voice should be heard, the voices of artists, of *savants*, of men of letters, of patriots, of the faithful, of women, of soldiers, and . . . in an appealing solo, the voice of Reims."[1]

Reims has had various opportunities for expressing her feeling, and we know what she thinks. Reims thinks she has suffered too much to be called upon to suffer more. Reims, who means to build up her ruins, will not understand that an exception should be made in respect of that, the saddest, the most tragic, the most revolting of them all. Reims thinks she has not deserved the fate of keeping her Cathedral disfigured, and with its glory diminished. Reims declares that she is too proud of it, and that she loves it too well, ever to resign herself to seeing it less beautiful.

[1] See H. Lavedan. *Illustration* of 13th March, 1915.

APPENDIX A

PROCLAMATION

APPENDIX A

PROCLAMATION

IN the event of an action being fought to-day or in the immediate future in the neighbourhood of Reims or in the town itself, the inhabitants are notified that they must remain absolutely calm, and not attempt in any way to take part in the battle. They must not attempt to attack either isolated soldiers or detachments of the German army. It is formally forbidden to erect barricades, or pull up the pavement of streets, for the purpose of hampering the movement of troops, or, in a word, to do anything whatever which might in any way be injurious to the German army.

In order to ensure adequately the safety of the troops, and to answer for the calm behaviour of the population of Reims, the persons named below have been taken as hostages by the high command of the German Army. These hostages will be hung upon the slightest attempt at disorder. In addition the city will be completely or partially burned and the inhabitants hung, if any infraction whatsoever of the above orders is committed.

On the other hand, if the city remains absolutely tranquil and calm, the hostages and inhabitants will be under the safeguard of the German Army.

By Order of the German Authority,

DR. LANGLET, Mayor.

REIMS, 12 *Sept.*, 1914.

(Then follows a list of the hostages.)

179

APPENDIX B

PROTESTS BY LEARNED
AND OTHER SOCIETIES
AND AUTHORS

APPENDIX B

PROTESTS BY LEARNED AND OTHER SOCIETIES AND AUTHORS

" THE *Académie Française*, in the name of French civilization and of human civilization, stigmatizes . . . the incendiaries of Louvain University and Reims Cathedral, the men who, if they could, would also have burned Notre-Dame of Paris."

(At the session of the 22nd October, 1914.)

" The *Académie des Beaux-Arts* protests against the rage of destruction of our enemies and the outrages which they have inflicted upon one of the most sublime productions of the French genius, the Cathedral of Reims, the monument which best displays those traits which belong to the artistic genius of our race."

" Abominable attack upon a monument which belongs not to France alone, but to the whole world !

" The civilized world was seized with stupor in learning of this monstrous crime, the shame of which will remain for ever upon those who in cold blood premeditated it."

(*Société des Antiquaires de France*, 28th September, 1914.)

" If the *Académie des Inscriptions et Belles-Lettres* has not before this protested against those abominable acts and

183

that impious destruction . . . such as the burning of Louvain, and the bombardment of the Cathedrals of Malines and Reims, it is because such acts of violence appeared to have been sufficiently reprobated and branded by the indignation which arose on all sides.

" But to-day the appeal of German *savants* to public opinion, for the purpose of misleading it, does not permit us any longer to keep silence."

(At the session of the 30th October, 1914.)

" The *Société française d'Archéologie* associates itself with the indignant protests of the civilized world against the savage and methodical bombardment of the Cathedral of Reims ; curses the odious German vandalism, proud of a victory gained over ancient stones, and deplores the irreparable ravages caused by the premeditated burning of this wonderful edifice."

(2nd October, 1914.)

" The *Société française des Architectes* raises an indignant protest against the unjustifiable destruction of one of the most precious jewels of our Thirteenth century national architecture, the Cathedral of Reims, the pride of our France, the admiration of the entire world."

(23rd September, 1914.)

" Absurd and criminal act, which staggers the reason, and condemns our enemies to the execration of all who think or feel, or who love and venerate beauty."

(*Société des Antiquaires Diplômés.*)

Appendix B

" *The Académie des Sciences Morales et Politiques* fulfils a duty of its functions in noting, in the acts of the German Government, a retrogression to the state of barbarism."
(At the session of the 31st October, 1914.)

" However irreparable have been the crimes which they have committed in Belgium, the ruin of Reims Cathedral, by a premeditated and prolonged bombardment, has almost thrown into the shade these former acts of savagery. It will be proclaimed for all time as a crime against humanity."
(*Society of Antiquaries of London.*)

" The Administrative Council of the *Touring Club of France*, in the name of its 140,000 members, consigns to the execration of the civilized world the abominable crime of these modern barbarians." (28th September, 1914.)

" History will say that our most sacred national sanctuary, the Cathedral of Reims, that marvel of our French art, has been destroyed in cold blood, without military motive, and for the sole purpose of injuring and bringing to ruin a treasury of souvenirs and beauty."
(*Académie de Médecine*, 27th November, 1914.)

" Monstrous and baffling crime, which has put into mourning the soul of every man of intellect through the world." (*Cercle d'Art Anversois*, of Scalden.)

" Abominable crime against one of the most august witnesses of the history and genius of France."
(*Société de l'Histoire de l'Art Français.*)

185

The Cathedral of Reims

" We have learned with horror of the destruction which has menaced Reims Cathedral, a temple rendered sacred to every civilized man, not only by its triumphant artistic beauty, but by its association with so many historic events in the life of France."

(Irish Deputation to the Cardinal Archbishop of Paris, 30th April, 1915.)

" *The Imperial Archæological Society of Moscow* is full of indignation in the presence of this barbarous and sacrilegious act : the destruction of the venerable and splendid Cathedral of Reims, that jewel of mediæval art, where the ancient kings of France, at their consecration, took their oath on the Gospel."

" The *Conseil de la fédération des églises protestantes de France*, in the name of French Protestantism generally, is, with the whole of humanity, indignant at the destruction of Louvain and the bombardment of Reims Cathedral."

" Act of barbarism which strikes humanity at large in one of the most noble monuments of its moral and artistic greatness."

(Protest of Swiss writers, artists and *savants*, bearing a thousand signatures.)

" Crime which will soil Prussianism for ever before the incorruptible tribunal of history."

(The Academies, Higher Schools and Artistic Societies of Portugal, 4th October, 1914.)

" In spite of the horror aroused throughout the world by the devastation of Malines and Louvain, the German armies have just ravaged the Cathedral of Reims. To this act of murder against human genius the best minds in every country ought to reply with a cry of revolt which should brand the sacrilegious destroyers."

> (Protest of British artists and writers—three hundred signatures.)

" The representatives of Universities, Academies, Art Institutions, Museums and Artistic Societies of the entire world, affiliated to the International Association of the Fine Arts of Rome, protest strongly against the disregard of international conventions consecrated by a world-wide cult of beauty and violated by the bombardment of one of the world's greatest Gothic works of architecture and sculpture."

> (*L'Eclair*, of the 28th September, 1914.)

" In the presence of such acts reason is baffled, and the artistic soul of France is shocked, but that of architects suffers and waxes indignant perhaps more violently than all the others.

" Habituated to the veneration of the admirable relics of fine epochs in our history, we cannot contain the emotion, the anger and the disgust which the abominable crime committed by the German hordes provokes in us."

> (*La Société des Architectes Diplomés*.)

" It is impossible to express in moderate terms the feelings with which British architects have learned of the pitiless destruction of noble monuments, such as Reims Cathedral, which up to now had escaped the ravages of time. These acts of barbarism are a proof that the German aggression is an attack upon the common civilization of Europe."

> (*Royal Institute of British Architects*.)

PROTESTS BY AUTHORS

" A sword thrust at the heart of France. Base and cowardly wrong brutally thrown in her face !

" The civilized world will answer with a cry of horror the savage barbarism of the Twentieth-century Huns."

(A. de Mun, *Echo de Paris*, 22nd September, 1914.)

" Having found on his road Catholic Louvain, William II abolishes it ; then he sought Reims.

" There is at once the cradle of Catholicism among the Gauls, the cradle of French royalty, and the cradle of the nation. . . . Reims, set apart by the magnificence of an art which is the flower of our soil, and which can only be plagiarized elsewhere, is all that, and above all, it is the heart of our nationality.

" That is why the German Emperor burned the Cathedral of Reims, the Church of St. Rémi, and the basilica of coronation."

Frédéric Masson, *Echo de Paris*, 25th September, 1914).

" It is a declaration of war against all that is greatest in the world that the generals of the German Emperor have just launched, in turning their guns upon the spot where Clovis received the inheritance of Latin civilization, on that dazzling House of divine beauty. . . .

" Into those stones which the Prussians are shelling they are not putting the immobility of death. They will

188

only be more thrilling, better charged with life, more sacred. . . .

" Holy Cathedral of Reims, all mutilated as you are, you yet remain to the mind's eye our national relic."

(Maurice Barrès, *Echo de Paris*, 21st September, 1914.)

" Notwithstanding their grotesquely absurd pretexts, their impudent denials, what they wanted to destroy here was the very heart of old France.

" . . . The great barbarism has passed there,—the modern barbarism from across the Rhine, a thousand times worse than the old, because it is stupidly and outrageously satisfied with itself, and in consequence, fundamental, incurable, positive, and fated, unless it be crushed, to cast over the world a sinister night of eclipse."

(Pièrre Loti, see *Illustration*, 21st November, 1914.)

" It was especially as the great work of piety and art of our fathers that the hate of an enemy, dastardly, envious and savage, fell with fury upon the essential monument of our most sacred history. In firing upon the sanctuary of Reims, Germany has fired upon the baptism of Clovis, upon the standard of Joan of Arc, upon the oil of consecration of Hugh Capet and his successors, upon the greatest figures of the French monarchy, for all these *souvenirs* scattered in the hearts of numberless Frenchmen, were assembled under your beautiful arches, to-day in ruins."

(Duke of Orleans, Letter to Cardinal Luçon.)

The Cathedral of Reims

" It is the Catholic soul of France, the national soul, which they wanted to wound, in falling upon this body of beauty. And, without doubt, they thought they would kill it.

" But they have deceived themselves. Life may arise from the stake. Did it not arise from the stake of Joan of Arc ? . . .

" Little birds of Reims [an allusion to a pretty custom at the coronation ceremony] to-day, with the roofs caved in by shells, and the windows broken, you no longer stay. Go, go to the east, to the other cathedral, to the spire already injured, it also, by German guns, go and salute the great birds of Alsace, the storks of Strasbourg ! . . . Tell them that the crime of Reims has rejuvenated the Pact of St. Rémi, and that France is about to resume her march towards her immortal ideal. . . ."

(Mgr. Baudrillart, Sermon at Ste Clothilde.)

" The Germans have a systematic code of destruction, of terror, and of instruments to put it in force and by order, contrary to all the treaties and conventions concerning the laws of war, a code absolutely devoid of honour, of decency or of pity."

(Whitney Warren, Letter to the Institute of
Arts at New York, à propos of the bom-
bardment of Reims Cathedral.)

" Let our soldiers take their Emperor alive, bring him barefoot and with a rope round his neck, to the ruins of the basilica, and there, on his degraded face, let the executioner strike the abject race which bombards cathedrals."

(Louis Bertrand, Les Annales, 7th Sept., 1914.)

" What is happening awakens a feeling throughout the world : henceforth men will speak of the fall of Reims as they speak of the fall of Constantinople, and will date from it. . . . How somnolent we became, and what blows awake us ! "

(A. Rodin.)

" The criminal act accomplished at Reims by the savage enemy of France is a provocation to the whole world. It characterizes an army, a nation, a reign. I am as much dismayed at it as the best of Frenchmen."

(The Prince of Monaco.)

" Never will anything excuse the attack upon these great works of art. Everything that is said at Berlin and Vienna to explain it has but added lying to error. The fires of Louvain and Reims are historic crimes. The sacrilege was open and by order."

(Em. Verhaeren, Belgian poet, *Le Temps*, 24th January, 1915.)

" They have covered themselves with undying infamy, and the German name has become execrable throughout the thinking world."

(A. France.)

" The destruction of the basilica of Reims, incomparable monument of piety, art and historical recollections, is an odious blasphemy against God, the Father of us all, and denotes the absence from its authors of every religious and human sentiment."

(A. Lévy, Grand Rabbi of France.)

The Cathedral of Reims

" Woe to you who devastate, and who have not yet been devastated, who plunder, and have not yet been plundered. When you have finished devastating and plundering, you in your turn will be devastated and plundered. . . . (Is. xxxiii. 1.) "   (E. Cohen, Grand Rabbi of Lille.)

" Before their flight
The Imperial eagles
In truth should have seen
There, down below in the depth of the night,
With burning arms, the old Cathedral
Spread forth their shame to the future."

(Em. Verhaeren.)

APPENDIX C

LIST OF SHELLS KNOWN TO
HAVE STRUCK THE CATHEDRAL

O

APPENDIX C

LIST OF SHELLS KNOWN TO HAVE STRUCK THE CATHEDRAL

(FROM THE 4TH OF SEPTEMBER, 1914, TO THE 17TH OF SEPTEMBER, 1918)

1914

4th	September		..	..	.. 1
17th	,,		..	..	.. 3
18th	,,		..	..	.. 13
19th	,,	(the fire)	..		.. 25
24th	,,		..	..	.. 3
12th	October ..		..	..	.. 1
11th	November		..	..	.. 1
12th	,,		..	..	.. 1
17th	,,		..	..	.. 1
22nd	,,		..	..	.. 2
23rd	,,		..	..	.. 3
24th	,,		..	..	.. 1
26th	,,		..	..	.. 5
28th	,,		..	..	.. 2
4th	December		..	..	.. 1

1915

18th	February		..	..	.. 2
21st	,,		..	..	.. 7

22nd February	..	..	..	3
26th ,,	..	..	..	2
2nd March	..	..	..	1
24th ,,	..	..	..	1
8th April	..	..	..	3
1st June	..	..	..	2
15th ,,	..	..	..	6
27th ,,	..	..	..	1
3rd July	..	..	..	1
21st ,,	..	..	..	2
19th October	..	..	..	1

1916

2nd April	..	..	..	3
11th July	..	..	..	1
27th October	..	..	..	3

1917

16th April	..	..	..	14
19th ,,	..	..	..	20
21st ,,	..	..	..	2
24th ,,	..	..	..	?
14th June	..	..	..	1
28th ,,	..	..	..	3
29th ,,	..	..	..	2
26th July	..	..	..	1
30th ,,	..	..	..	1
13th August	..	..	..	3
23rd ,,	..	..	..	2
28th ,,	..	..	..	1
18th December	..	..	..	1

Appendix C

16th	February	..	..	..	1
18th	March	..	..	..	1
21st	,,	..	..	..	4

Thus, at the date of the evacuation, 159 shells had been accounted for, 42 before the fire, and 117 after.

From the 21st March to the 25th June, 1918, information is lacking.

Starting from the 25th of June, M. le Chef d'Escadron Lexa, town major of Reims, noted in his daily reports from the gendarmerie :—

25th	June	..	..	..	.. 4
26th	July	..	..	..	.. 3
29th	,,	..	..	..	.. 15
31st	,,	..	..	..	.. 5
7th	August	..	..	..	.. 3
8th	,,	..	..	..	.. 10
12th	,,	..	..	..	.. 15
14th	,,	..	..	..	.. 6
17th	,,	..	..	..	.. 2
20th	,,	..	..	..	.. 23
25th	,,	..	..	..	.. 10
7th	September	..	..	..	.. 15
17th	,,	..	..	..	.. 17

Total   .. 128

The Cathedral has thus received (159+128) 287 shells noted, without counting the awful day of the 24th April, 1917, when such terrible ravages were made, but when the shots could not be counted one by one ; nor the three months in the spring of 1918 (21st March to 25th June), when there was no one to take the sinister day's record.

As for the town, if one wishes to pursue to the end the reckoning of the days of bombardment indicated on page 24, one must add 194 to the figure of 857, up to the 24th March, 1918 ; for, after the evacuation, up to the 5th October, there was shelling every day. The number therefore should be $857 + 194 = 1051$.

PRINTED BY WILLIAM BRENDON AND SON, LTD.
PLYMOUTH, ENGLAND